Virtual Reality and the Metaverse

How AR and VR are Shaping the Digital World A Look at the Future of Immersive Tech, NFTs, and Web3

Greyson Chesterfield

COPYRIGHT

DISCLAIMER

The information provided in this book is for general informational purposes only. All content in this book reflects the author's views and is based on their research, knowledge, and experiences. The author and publisher make no representations or warranties of any kind concerning the completeness, accuracy, reliability, suitability, or availability of the information contained herein.

This book is not intended to be a substitute for professional advice, diagnosis, or treatment. Readers should seek professional advice for any specific concerns or conditions. The author and publisher disclaim any liability or responsibility for any direct, indirect, incidental, or consequential loss or damage arising from the use of the information contained in this book.

Chapter 1: Introduction to Immersive Technologies

1.1 What is Immersive Technology?

Immersive technology is an umbrella term that encompasses a broad range of technologies that create highly engaging digital experiences by integrating virtual or augmented elements into the physical world. These technologies—augmented reality (AR), virtual reality (VR), and mixed reality (MR)—work together to break down the boundaries between the digital and physical realms, enabling users to interact with both in highly dynamic, intuitive, and immersive ways. Immersive technologies are not just about virtual experiences; they represent a complete shift in how we perceive and engage with the digital world.

At the heart of immersive technology lies AR, VR, and MR. These technologies differ in terms of their engagement with the physical world and their core objectives. Let's examine each one to understand its individual characteristics and their collective impact on industries.

Augmented Reality (AR)

Augmented Reality blends the real world with digital information, allowing users to view and interact with digital elements that are overlaid on the real world. Unlike VR, where the user is fully immersed in a digital environment, AR enhances the user's perception of the real world by integrating digital content such as images, videos, 3D objects, and sounds.

For example, AR is commonly used in mobile applications where digital objects are placed on the screen, but users can still see their surroundings. One of the most well-known AR applications is *Pokémon Go*, where players use their phones to hunt virtual

Pokémon, which appear to coexist within the physical environment.

In the professional world, AR is making significant strides in industries like healthcare, retail, automotive, and education. In healthcare, surgeons are using AR to overlay crucial information onto a patient's body, guiding them during complex surgeries. Retailers like IKEA use AR in their apps to let customers visualize how furniture will look in their homes before making a purchase.

Virtual Reality (VR)

Virtual Reality creates a fully immersive experience where the user is placed into a completely simulated environment, cutting them off from the real world. This is accomplished through the use of specialized headsets, such as Oculus Rift, HTC Vive, and PlayStation VR, which are equipped with motion sensors, trackers, and sometimes haptic feedback devices to enhance immersion.

In VR, the user can interact with and manipulate the environment using controllers or hand-tracking systems. For instance, in gaming, VR allows users to physically interact with the virtual world—picking up objects, dodging enemies, and even fighting with realistic motion-sensing controllers.

However, VR is far more than just gaming. It is being used in simulation training for pilots, military personnel, and doctors, allowing them to practice critical skills in a safe, controlled environment. Furthermore, VR offers a completely new approach to remote collaboration, with virtual offices and meeting rooms offering a more interactive and collaborative alternative to traditional video conferencing.

Mixed Reality (MR)

Mixed Reality combines the elements of both AR and VR to create environments where the real and virtual worlds interact in real-time. MR allows virtual objects to not only coexist with the real world but also interact with it. This creates a more fluid and realistic experience where the user can interact with both physical and digital objects simultaneously.

Microsoft's HoloLens is a leading example of mixed reality, allowing users to interact with holograms that respond to their movements and gestures. For example, a designer using HoloLens can manipulate 3D models of products as if they were tangible, or a surgeon can use MR to project 3D images of a patient's organs during surgery to make more precise incisions.

The Impact of Immersive Technology on Industries

Immersive technologies are transforming industries across the board. Below, we explore how AR, VR, and MR are reshaping various sectors.

1. Healthcare

In healthcare, immersive technologies are revolutionizing training, patient care, and surgery. VR is being used to create highly realistic simulations for training medical professionals, allowing them to perform procedures in a controlled, risk-free environment. This not only saves time and money but also reduces the risk of human error in real-world situations.

In surgical applications, AR is helping surgeons by overlaying vital information directly onto the patient's body or providing 3D models of organs. This capability improves the accuracy of operations and reduces complications.

MR, particularly with devices like the HoloLens, is also playing a vital role in medical training and surgery. Surgeons can visualize 3D models of patient organs and tissues overlaid onto their body, providing them with an extra layer of information to make better decisions.

2. Education and Training

In the education sector, immersive technology is enhancing the learning experience by providing interactive, engaging, and hands-on learning environments. VR is used for virtual field trips, allowing students to visit historical landmarks, museums, or even outer space without leaving the classroom. This approach enhances engagement, making learning more fun and memorable.

Furthermore, AR is being used in classrooms to help students visualize complex concepts. For instance, an AR app can project a 3D model of the solar system in a student's desk, allowing them to interact with it and learn in a more engaging manner.

3. Retail

The retail industry is also benefiting from immersive technologies. With AR, customers can virtually try on clothes or view how a product will look in their homes before purchasing. For instance, apps like Sephora's

AR makeup try-on feature let customers see how different cosmetics would look on their skin without ever needing to test them physically.

Additionally, VR is being used in retail to offer immersive shopping experiences. Virtual stores allow customers to browse products, interact with store layouts, and even participate in promotions—all within a completely virtual environment.

4. Automotive

In the automotive industry, AR, VR, and MR are being used in various stages of production, design, and sales. In design, VR allows automotive manufacturers to create virtual prototypes of vehicles and conduct real-time testing, saving on the costs and time of physical production.

On the sales front, MR is being used to enhance the car-buying experience by allowing customers to explore virtual car models and customize features using interactive holograms. AR is also being utilized in automotive head-up displays, where drivers see critical information such as speed, navigation, and hazard warnings directly projected onto their windshields, improving safety and reducing distraction.

5. Real Estate and Architecture

In real estate, immersive technologies are making it easier for buyers to explore properties from anywhere in the world. VR tours allow prospective buyers to walk through homes and buildings without physically visiting them. This has proven invaluable, particularly in the context of the COVID-19 pandemic, where physical tours were restricted.

In architecture, MR is helping designers and architects visualize building projects. Using MR, architects can interact with 3D models of buildings, allowing them to see and manipulate designs in real-time. This process not only speeds up design but also ensures that potential issues are identified before construction begins.

1.2 A Brief History of AR and VR

The roots of AR and VR can be traced back decades, with key milestones marking the evolution of immersive technologies. From early theoretical ideas to today's advanced, user-friendly devices, AR and VR have undergone significant transformations. Let's explore the history and milestones that have shaped these technologies.

The Birth of Virtual Reality

The idea of VR has its origins in the 1960s, long before the technology became widely known. The first VR head-mounted display (HMD) was developed by Ivan Sutherland in 1968. Called the "Sword of Damocles," this early VR system was a cumbersome, room-sized setup that used a head-mounted display to show basic 3D graphics. Although primitive, it laid the groundwork for the future of VR.

In the 1980s, VR began to gain more attention with the development of systems like VPL Research's "DataGlove" and "EyePhone." These devices allowed users to interact with virtual environments using their hands and provided a more immersive experience than previous technologies.

During the 1990s, VR technology became more accessible to the public through the development of commercial VR systems, such as Nintendo's Virtual Boy. However, these early systems suffered from limited graphics and high costs, which prevented them from gaining widespread adoption.

The early 2000s saw a resurgence in interest in VR, driven by the growth of gaming and advancements in computing power. Technologies like the Oculus Rift, released in 2012, finally brought high-quality VR experiences to the masses. Oculus, acquired by Facebook in 2014, has since played a leading role in popularizing VR for gaming, entertainment, and beyond.

The Rise of Augmented Reality

While VR was making waves, AR began to take shape in parallel. The term "augmented reality" was first coined by Tom Caudell in the early 1990s, though the technology dates back even further. Early AR systems required bulky equipment and were mostly used for research or military purposes.

A breakthrough in AR came in 2009 with the release of *Layar*, one of the first AR mobile apps. This app allowed users to see AR overlays through their smartphones by using the phone's camera and GPS to display location-based information. As smartphones became more powerful and ubiquitous, AR began to find applications in gaming, marketing, and entertainment.

In 2016, Pokémon Go took AR mainstream, creating a global phenomenon where players interacted with virtual characters overlaid on the real world. This marked the beginning of widespread public interest in AR applications for entertainment and beyond.

The Current State of Immersive Technologies

Today, immersive technologies are at the cusp of mainstream adoption. The development of more affordable and powerful hardware—such as the Oculus Quest 2, HoloLens, and Magic Leap—has made AR and VR more accessible to consumers, while advances in 5G connectivity are set to accelerate the adoption of these technologies in industries like healthcare, automotive, and entertainment.

In addition, the emergence of the Metaverse—a collective virtual shared space that incorporates AR, VR, and MR—has captured the imagination of both tech enthusiasts and industry leaders. As we move toward a more interconnected digital future, immersive technologies will play an increasingly important role in how we live, work, and interact with each other.

The journey of AR and VR from their conceptual beginnings to their current form reflects the rapid pace of technological advancement and the growing importance of immersive experiences in our digital lives.

Chapter 2: Understanding Virtual Reality (VR)

2.1 What Is Virtual Reality?

Virtual Reality (VR) is a groundbreaking immersive technology that creates a completely digital experience, isolating users from the real world and placing them into a computer-generated environment. Unlike other technologies, such as Augmented Reality (AR) and Mixed Reality (MR), VR fully immerses the user in a virtual world, using sophisticated equipment like headsets, motion controllers, and tracking sensors. VR not only provides an experience that feels realistic but also enables interaction with the virtual environment in ways that mimic real-world interactions.

At its core, VR's goal is to trick the brain into believing that the virtual environment is real. Through sensory cues like sight, sound, and sometimes even touch (via haptic feedback), VR systems stimulate the brain to perceive and engage with a virtual space as if it were an actual, physical location. This creates a sense of presence—an important factor in enhancing immersion and ensuring that users are completely engaged in their digital experience.

Difference Between VR and Other Immersive Technologies

While VR shares similarities with other immersive technologies such as AR and MR, it is important to differentiate VR from these technologies. Here's a breakdown of key differences:

Virtual Reality (VR):

- Fully immersive experience, disconnecting users from the real world.

- The environment is entirely virtual and computer-generated.

- Requires specialized equipment such as VR headsets and controllers to interact with the digital world.

- Common applications include gaming, training simulations, and virtual tourism.

Augmented Reality (AR):

- Enhances the real world by overlaying digital elements on top of the physical environment.

- Users remain aware of and engaged with the real world while interacting with digital elements.

- Typically experienced through mobile devices like smartphones or AR glasses.

- Common applications include navigation, gaming (e.g., Pokémon Go), and product visualization.

Mixed Reality (MR):

- Blends both the real and virtual worlds, allowing them to interact in real-time.

- Unlike AR, where digital objects are just overlaid on the real world, MR allows virtual objects to be placed in real-world environments, where they can interact with physical objects.

- MR often requires specialized devices like Microsoft HoloLens.

- Common applications include industrial design, education, and collaborative workspaces.

While all three technologies—VR, AR, and MR—share the goal of creating immersive experiences, VR's focus on fully immersing users into a completely virtual world sets it apart from its counterparts, which blend virtual elements with the real world.

Key Components of VR

To understand how VR works, it's important to familiarize yourself with the key components that make the experience possible. These include:

1. VR Headsets:

The headset is arguably the most critical component of any VR system. It provides the visual display of the virtual environment and is equipped with sensors to track the user's head movements. Popular headsets include:

- **Oculus Quest 2**: A standalone VR headset that doesn't require an external PC or console, offering freedom of movement and flexibility.

- **HTC Vive Pro**: A premium VR headset known for its excellent resolution, tracking, and compatibility with external devices.

- **PlayStation VR**: A headset designed for Sony's PlayStation console, delivering an accessible VR experience for gaming enthusiasts.

These headsets come with built-in screens (usually OLED or LCD), offering high resolutions that ensure crisp, clear visuals in the virtual environment. They use motion sensors like gyroscopes, accelerometers, and sometimes external tracking sensors to track the user's head movements, ensuring that the virtual world reacts in real-time as the user moves.

2. Motion Controllers:
Controllers are essential for interacting with the virtual environment. They track hand movements, allowing users to manipulate objects, navigate, and even perform actions such as shooting or picking up virtual items. Some controllers come equipped with haptic feedback, providing tactile sensations that simulate the feeling of touch in the virtual world. Popular VR controllers include the **Oculus Touch controllers** and **HTC Vive controllers**, which provide

intuitive inputs for users to interact with their VR surroundings.

3. Tracking Sensors:

Tracking sensors are responsible for monitoring the user's movements within a defined physical space, such as a room or a larger area. These sensors help translate the user's physical actions into virtual actions in real-time, maintaining the sense of immersion. External sensors like **Lighthouse trackers** (used with HTC Vive) or **Oculus external cameras** enable accurate tracking of head and controller movements. Some systems, like the **Oculus Quest 2**, also incorporate inside-out tracking, using cameras on the headset itself to track movement.

4. Audio Equipment:

Sound plays a crucial role in enhancing the VR experience, providing auditory cues that make the virtual world feel more lifelike. Many VR headsets come with built-in audio systems, such as spatial audio, which adjusts sound depending on the direction the user is facing. Headphones or earphones can also be used for a more immersive experience, especially in applications like gaming and virtual tourism.

5. Haptic Feedback Devices:

Haptic feedback devices provide physical sensations to users, enhancing the realism of VR interactions. These can include vibrations in controllers or wearable suits that simulate the feeling of touch, such as when you're holding an object or touching something in the virtual world. Haptic feedback helps increase the immersion and realism of VR experiences.

2.2 Types of VR

There are different types of VR systems, each offering varying levels of immersion, cost, and accessibility. The main categories of VR are:

Room-Scale VR

Room-scale VR offers the highest level of immersion by allowing users to physically move around within a defined space (usually a room). The virtual environment adapts to the user's movement, creating an interactive experience where users can walk, crouch, or even jump as they explore the virtual world.

To enable room-scale VR, external tracking sensors or base stations (such as the **HTC Vive base stations**) are placed around the room to detect the user's movements. These sensors track the position of the headset and controllers in 3D space, ensuring that the user's actions translate into the virtual environment.

Room-scale VR is particularly useful for applications that require large amounts of space, such as VR gaming and simulations. It is often used in high-end VR systems like the **HTC Vive Pro** or **Valve Index**, which provide an expansive and immersive experience.

Mobile VR

Mobile VR provides a more portable VR experience by using smartphones as the primary computing device. Mobile VR headsets, such as the **Samsung Gear VR** or **Google Cardboard**, utilize the smartphone's screen and processing power to deliver VR content.

While mobile VR isn't as powerful as high-end room-scale VR systems, it is much more affordable and accessible, making it ideal for casual use. Mobile VR headsets are lightweight and can be used anywhere, offering users the ability to enjoy virtual content on-the-go. Mobile VR is most commonly used for gaming, video consumption, and interactive apps.

Standalone VR

Standalone VR systems like the **Oculus Quest 2** offer a self-contained experience, eliminating the need for external computers, consoles, or sensors. These systems have built-in processors, storage, and displays, allowing users to enjoy a fully immersive VR experience without additional hardware.

Standalone VR is a game-changer in terms of accessibility and ease of use, providing a high-quality VR experience in a compact and wireless package. Devices like the **Oculus Quest 2** are popular for gaming, fitness apps, and interactive VR experiences, offering the convenience of portability combined with impressive performance.

Standalone VR offers the freedom of room-scale VR while being more accessible and affordable than traditional tethered systems. Its wireless nature also makes it more user-friendly, as there are no cords or external sensors to set up, making it ideal for casual users and professionals alike.

2.3 How VR Is Used in the Real World

Virtual reality is no longer a niche technology used only in gaming; it has evolved into a transformative tool that is reshaping industries across the globe. Below are some key real-world applications of VR:

1. Gaming and Entertainment

VR has had the most significant impact on the gaming industry, providing immersive experiences that traditional gaming cannot match. With VR, players can enter a game world as if they were physically present, interacting with characters and environments in ways that feel more natural and engaging.

Popular games like **Half-Life: Alyx**, **Beat Saber**, and **Resident Evil 7: Biohazard** have taken advantage of VR's capabilities to offer players a more intense and interactive experience. Additionally, VR gaming is increasingly being integrated into theme parks and entertainment centers, offering hyper-realistic rides and experiences that are accessible to the masses.

2. Healthcare and Medical Training

In healthcare, VR is being used for training medical professionals, offering realistic simulations of surgeries and medical procedures. Surgeons can practice complex surgeries in a virtual environment without putting patients at risk. This allows for repeated practice and better preparation for real-world procedures.

Beyond training, VR is also used in therapeutic settings, such as exposure therapy for treating PTSD and phobias. Patients can be immersed in controlled virtual environments that help them confront their fears in a safe and gradual manner. Furthermore, VR is being used in pain management, where patients undergoing medical procedures can be distracted by immersive environments that reduce their perception of pain.

3. Education and Training

Education is another sector that stands to benefit immensely from VR. Students can engage in virtual field trips, visiting historical sites or exploring outer space, all from the comfort of the classroom. VR provides a more engaging and hands-on learning experience, improving retention and understanding of complex subjects.

For training purposes, VR offers realistic simulations for a variety of industries. Whether it's aviation, military, or engineering, professionals can practice and refine their skills in a controlled environment, improving proficiency and reducing training costs.

4. Architecture and Real Estate

In architecture and real estate, VR is changing how designs are visualized and presented. Architects can create 3D models of buildings and allow clients to "walk through" these designs before construction begins. This helps clients get a better sense of scale, layout, and design, allowing for real-time feedback and revisions.

In real estate, VR is being used for virtual property tours. Prospective buyers can view properties remotely, interacting with different rooms and layouts from the comfort of their homes. This has become especially popular in the wake of the COVID-19 pandemic, where in-person viewings became restricted.

5. Remote Work and Collaboration

With the rise of remote work, VR is providing innovative solutions for team collaboration and virtual offices. VR platforms like **AltspaceVR** and **Spatial** allow people to meet in virtual environments, interact with digital avatars, and collaborate on projects in a way that feels more natural than traditional video conferencing.

This technology is particularly valuable for teams working across different locations and time zones, as it helps bridge the gap created by physical distance and enhances the sense of presence in digital meetings.

2.4 Hands-On Project: Building Your First VR Space

Creating a VR environment is an exciting and rewarding endeavor, especially for those who want to dive into the world of VR development. In this section, we will walk through the process of setting up a simple VR space using **Unity**, one of the most popular game development platforms for VR.

Step 1: Setting Up Unity for VR Development

1. **Download and Install Unity**
Visit the Unity website and download the latest version of Unity Hub. Once installed, open Unity Hub and create a new project. Select the 3D

template, as we'll be working with a 3D environment.

2. **Install the VR SDK**

   For our VR project, we need to install the VR SDK for your headset. If you're using the **Oculus Quest 2**, you'll need the **Oculus Integration** package from the Unity Asset Store. This package contains all the necessary tools to build VR applications for the Oculus platform.

Step 2: Creating a Simple VR Environment

1. **Create the Environment**

   Begin by creating a basic scene. You can add objects like a floor, walls, and a skybox to create a basic room. Use Unity's built-in 3D objects to add a floor (using a plane), walls (using cubes), and a simple light source to brighten up your environment.

2. **Add the VR Camera**

   Unity has a special camera setup for VR. Replace the main camera in the scene with the VR camera prefab provided in the Oculus Integration package. This camera will simulate the user's viewpoint and allow them to look around the virtual space.

3. **Add Interaction**

   To make the VR environment interactive, you can add simple interactions like grabbing objects. Unity supports the use of controllers for object interaction, so you can set up an interaction script to allow users to pick up, throw, and manipulate objects in the environment.

Step 3: Testing and Debugging

1. **Deploy to Your VR Headset**

   Connect your VR headset to your computer and build the project. You can run the VR environment directly from Unity to test how it behaves in real-time. Make sure to test the movement, interactions, and overall user experience.

2. **Debug and Improve**

   Test the environment thoroughly and debug any issues that arise. You can adjust the scale, interaction mechanics, and visual elements to improve the overall experience.

By the end of this project, you will have a basic VR environment where you can move around and interact with simple objects. This project will provide a solid foundation for more advanced VR development.

Chapter 3: Exploring Augmented Reality (AR)

3.1 What Is Augmented Reality?

Augmented Reality (AR) is an immersive technology that enhances the real world with digital elements, providing an interactive experience where virtual content is overlaid onto the physical environment. Unlike Virtual Reality (VR), which immerses users in a fully digital world, AR integrates computer-generated objects, sounds, and information into the user's view of the real world. This creates a unique experience that enhances perception and interaction in real-time.

AR can be experienced through a variety of devices, from smartphones and tablets to specialized AR glasses and headsets. What makes AR so powerful is its ability to blend the virtual and physical worlds seamlessly, allowing users to interact with both simultaneously. Whether you're using AR to visualize products before purchasing them, enhancing educational experiences, or navigating your way through unfamiliar environments, AR has proven to be a transformative technology across numerous industries.

The Difference Between AR and VR

Although both Augmented Reality (AR) and Virtual Reality (VR) fall under the umbrella of immersive technologies, they differ significantly in their core functionality, user experience, and applications. Below is a breakdown of the primary differences between AR and VR:

- **Immersion**:
    - ○ **AR**: Augmented Reality overlays digital elements onto the real world, allowing the user to remain aware of their physical surroundings. It enhances the real world with virtual content, but the user is still connected to the physical world.

- **VR**: Virtual Reality creates a fully immersive digital environment that isolates users from the real world. Through VR, users are transported into a completely computer-generated world, where physical surroundings are not visible or relevant.

- **Hardware**:

  - **AR**: AR is most commonly experienced through smartphones, tablets, and AR glasses (like Microsoft HoloLens or Magic Leap). These devices use cameras, sensors, and displays to integrate virtual objects into the physical world.

  - **VR**: VR requires specialized hardware such as headsets (Oculus Quest, HTC Vive, or PlayStation VR) that provide a fully immersive experience by blocking out the real world and displaying a digital environment.

- **Interactivity**:

  - **AR**: AR users interact with digital content in the context of the real world. They can touch, manipulate, or view virtual objects placed in physical space. For example, AR can overlay directions on a real-time view of the road or display product details in the environment.

- VR: VR interactions typically involve users navigating and manipulating the entire virtual world. These interactions can be hand-tracked or controller-based, and users often engage in dynamic tasks like gaming or simulations that require complete immersion.

- **Applications**:
  - AR: AR is used in navigation systems, retail experiences, education, and healthcare. It adds valuable digital layers to the real world, like giving directions on your phone screen or visualizing furniture in your living room.

  - VR: VR is primarily used in gaming, training simulations, and immersive storytelling. It is perfect for applications requiring full immersion in a virtual environment, such as flying simulations, medical training, or virtual tourism.

While VR offers complete immersion in a virtual world, AR allows users to interact with both real and virtual worlds in tandem. This dual interaction is where AR shines, enhancing real-world experiences with digital information that feels seamless and integrated.

Key Components of AR Devices and Software

The beauty of AR lies in its ability to bring digital content to life by merging the real and virtual worlds. To achieve this, AR relies on several critical components, including AR devices and software that enable the tracking, rendering, and interaction of virtual content with the real world.

1. AR Devices

AR devices are the hardware components that deliver the augmented experience. They vary depending on the level of immersion and the intended use. The main AR devices include:

- **Smartphones and Tablets**:
  These are the most common devices for AR experiences, as they come with built-in

cameras, processors, and displays. Popular apps like Pokémon Go, IKEA Place, and Snapchat filters leverage the camera and processing power of smartphones to deliver AR experiences. Most smartphones today come equipped with AR capabilities such as ARKit (for iOS) and ARCore (for Android), which enable the creation of AR content for a broad range of users.

- **AR Glasses and Headsets**:
  Devices like **Microsoft HoloLens**, **Magic Leap**, and **Google Glass** are designed specifically for augmented reality, offering hands-free experiences. These AR wearables combine spatial awareness with projection systems to display 3D virtual objects directly onto the user's field of view. AR glasses are ideal for enterprise applications like warehouse logistics, design work, and collaborative projects, where hands-free operation is critical.

- **Projectors**:
  Some AR applications use projectors to display virtual content onto physical surfaces. For example, a tabletop AR setup can project a 3D

object onto a surface, which users can interact with by touching or gesturing.

2. AR Software

AR software enables devices to render, track, and interact with digital content in a real-world environment. Key components of AR software include:

- **Computer Vision**:
  AR relies heavily on computer vision algorithms to interpret and track the user's environment. Computer vision enables AR systems to detect real-world objects, surfaces, and markers and track their position in real-time. Through object recognition and spatial mapping, AR software can accurately place virtual objects within a user's field of view, ensuring they appear to interact naturally with the real world.

- **3D Rendering**:
  AR requires the ability to render 3D models and animations that seamlessly blend into real-world environments. This involves applying depth and lighting effects to make virtual objects appear realistic. Software like Unity3D

and Unreal Engine are often used to create high-quality AR content, ensuring that digital models look as if they are physically present in the user's environment.

- **AR SDKs**:
  AR software development kits (SDKs) like **ARKit** (for iOS) and **ARCore** (for Android) provide developers with the tools needed to build AR applications. These SDKs include libraries for motion tracking, environmental understanding, and light estimation, making it easier to create AR experiences. With these SDKs, developers can implement features like marker-based AR (tracking specific images or objects) or markerless AR (where virtual objects are placed on any flat surface).

3.2 Real-World Applications of AR

Augmented Reality is not just a futuristic concept but a powerful tool that is transforming industries and everyday experiences. AR is increasingly finding applications in a wide variety of fields, from retail and navigation to entertainment, healthcare, and more.

Let's explore some of the most impactful and innovative uses of AR in the real world.

1. Retail and E-Commerce

In the retail sector, AR is revolutionizing the way consumers shop by allowing them to virtually try on products, visualize items in their homes, or interact with advertisements in new ways. Retailers are leveraging AR to enhance the customer experience, making it more interactive, personalized, and engaging.

- **Virtual Try-Ons**:
  AR enables users to try on clothes, makeup, or accessories virtually, without physically interacting with the product. For example, L'Oreal's AR app allows customers to try on makeup using their smartphone cameras, while **IKEA's AR app** lets customers see how furniture would look in their home before making a purchase. This reduces the uncertainty associated with online shopping and helps consumers make better purchasing decisions.

- **Interactive Shopping**:
  AR is transforming brick-and-mortar stores by offering interactive displays, virtual try-ons, and

in-store experiences that engage customers. For example, **Sephora's Virtual Artist** app allows users to see how makeup will look on their face through AR, without ever needing to apply it physically.

2. Navigation and Wayfinding

AR is also being used to revolutionize navigation systems, whether for driving, walking, or exploring unfamiliar locations. By overlaying directional arrows, points of interest, and real-time information onto the real-world environment, AR helps users navigate with ease and confidence.

- **AR Navigation Apps**: Apps like **Google Maps** have integrated AR to enhance their navigation features. With AR, users can hold up their smartphones and view step-by-step directions overlaid on the real-world street view, helping them navigate unfamiliar cities with ease.

- **Indoor Navigation**: AR is also being used for indoor navigation in large venues like airports, shopping malls, and museums. For example, **Wayfinder** in airports uses AR to guide travelers to their gates or luggage pickup areas, ensuring a smooth and stress-free journey.

3. Healthcare and Medicine

In healthcare, AR is being used to assist in surgeries, improve patient care, and train medical professionals. It offers doctors the ability to overlay 3D images of organs, tissues, and other critical data on the patient's body, providing a richer, more accurate understanding of the patient's condition.

- **Surgical Assistance**:
  Surgeons can use AR to view augmented visualizations of organs or bones during operations. For instance, **AccuVein**, an AR system, uses real-time imaging to help healthcare professionals locate veins for injections or blood draws.

- **Medical Training**:
  AR is also a powerful tool for training medical students, providing virtual dissections, 3D models of human anatomy, and simulations of complex surgeries. Students can interact with digital models of organs and body systems, gaining a deeper understanding of human anatomy and medical procedures.

4. Education and Training

AR is transforming education by providing interactive and engaging learning experiences that enhance student understanding and retention. Teachers can create immersive lessons by integrating virtual content into the physical world, creating dynamic learning environments.

- **Interactive Learning**:
  AR apps like **Google Expeditions** allow students to take virtual field trips to places like the Great Wall of China or the surface of Mars, providing a more interactive and engaging experience than traditional textbooks.

- **Skills Training**:
  In vocational and industrial training, AR is used to provide real-time guidance and step-by-step instructions. For example, **Microsoft HoloLens** is used to train workers on how to operate heavy machinery, overlaying instructions and diagnostics in their field of view to ensure tasks are performed correctly.

5. Entertainment and Gaming

The entertainment and gaming industries were among the first to adopt AR, offering consumers new ways to interact with their favorite franchises and content. AR games and experiences have become popular on mobile devices, and are now expanding into areas like live events and sports.

- **AR Games**:
  Games like **Pokémon Go** and **Harry Potter: Wizards Unite** have introduced millions to the potential of AR gaming, where users can interact with virtual characters and objects in the real world. These games encourage exploration, social interaction, and physical activity by combining real-world locations with digital gameplay.

- **Live Events and Sports**:
  AR is also being used in live events and sports broadcasts to enhance the viewer experience. For example, AR graphics are used during football games to overlay first-down markers or virtual replays onto the field, providing a richer viewing experience.

3.3 Building AR Experiences

Creating compelling AR experiences requires a blend of creativity, technical know-how, and the right tools. AR development can be accomplished using a variety of platforms and frameworks, with **ARKit** for iOS and **ARCore** for Android being the most popular options. These platforms provide developers with the necessary tools to create AR apps that leverage smartphone cameras, sensors, and powerful rendering engines.

Tools and Platforms for Building AR Experiences

- **ARKit (for iOS):**
  ARKit is Apple's framework for building AR applications on iOS devices. It provides a suite of tools for detecting surfaces, tracking motion, and rendering 3D objects. ARKit also includes features like facial recognition, image tracking, and environmental understanding, enabling developers to create immersive AR experiences.

- **ARCore (for Android):**
  ARCore is Google's equivalent to ARKit for Android devices. It enables developers to build AR applications by offering features like motion

tracking, environmental understanding, and light estimation. ARCore supports both Android smartphones and AR glasses, providing a versatile platform for AR development.

- **Unity and Unreal Engine**:
  For creating advanced AR experiences, both Unity and Unreal Engine are popular game development platforms that provide support for AR development. They offer built-in tools for 3D rendering, physics simulations, and animation, allowing developers to create high-quality AR applications.

3.4 Hands-On Project: Creating an AR App

In this section, we will guide you through the process of creating a simple AR app using **ARCore** for Android. This project will give you the fundamental understanding of AR development and how to implement basic AR features.

Step 1: Setting Up the Development Environment

1. **Install Android Studio**:
   To begin, you will need to install **Android**

Studio, which is the official integrated development environment (IDE) for Android development. You can download Android Studio from the official website.

2. **Install ARCore**:

   After setting up Android Studio, you need to install the ARCore SDK for Android. This can be done by adding the ARCore dependency to your project in Android Studio.

Step 2: Creating the AR App

1. **Create a New Project**:

   Open Android Studio and create a new project with a basic Activity template. Ensure that the project is set up to support ARCore by including the necessary dependencies in your app's build.gradle file.

2. **Add AR Session**:

   ARCore requires an AR session to handle camera inputs and environmental tracking. In the MainActivity, create an AR session object that will handle all AR-related operations, such as plane detection and object placement.

3. **Add AR Content:**

   Once the AR session is set up, you can start adding AR content. For this project, we'll place a simple 3D cube in the user's environment. You can use the built-in 3D models in Unity or create your own custom models for this purpose.

4. **Test and Debug:**

   After implementing the basic functionality, deploy the app to a compatible Android device (such as a Pixel or Samsung Galaxy). Test the AR features, ensuring the 3D object appears correctly in the real world.

Chapter 4: The Metaverse Explained

4.1 What Is the Metaverse?

The Metaverse, often hailed as the next frontier of the internet, is a rapidly evolving digital ecosystem of interconnected virtual worlds. The term "Metaverse" was first coined by Neal Stephenson in his 1992 science fiction novel *Snow Crash*, where it described a virtual world that users could enter using avatars. Today, the Metaverse represents more than just a single virtual world—it encompasses a collective digital space where users, through avatars, can interact, socialize, collaborate, and participate in a variety of activities.

At its core, the Metaverse is about creating a persistent, immersive, and fully interconnected virtual universe that blends virtual and physical realities. It's a convergence of several emerging technologies—augmented reality (AR), virtual reality (VR), mixed reality (MR), blockchain, artificial intelligence (AI), and digital economies—that allows users to engage with the digital world in ways that transcend traditional internet browsing.

While we are still in the early stages of its development, the Metaverse has the potential to revolutionize everything from entertainment and social networking to commerce, education, and even governance.

Definition and Key Principles

The Metaverse is an immersive, 3D virtual universe that spans multiple virtual worlds and allows for the creation and sharing of digital experiences. Here are some of the key principles that define the Metaverse:

- **Persistence**: The Metaverse is continuous and always "on." Virtual worlds do not pause or reset when users log off. They exist and evolve in real time, much like the real world. This persistence enables ongoing experiences that transcend individual sessions, ensuring that changes in the environment, user interactions, and digital assets remain intact.

- **Interoperability**: One of the fundamental ideas behind the Metaverse is the ability for different virtual worlds, apps, and platforms to seamlessly connect with one another. Users should be able to move from one virtual space to another without losing their identity, digital assets, or experiences. Interoperability will allow digital goods like NFTs, avatars, and even virtual currency to be used across multiple platforms, creating a unified digital economy.

- **Immersion**: The Metaverse aims to immerse users in a fully interactive 3D world, blending the real and digital. This immersion can be achieved through technologies such as VR, AR, and MR, where users can physically interact with virtual environments, objects, and other users, simulating a more lifelike experience than traditional 2D browsing.

- **Social Interaction**: At its heart, the Metaverse is about human connection. Whether through social media-like experiences, virtual concerts, multiplayer games, or virtual workplaces, the Metaverse aims to offer social spaces where people can meet, collaborate, play, and even build communities. These spaces are powered by avatars—digital representations of users—which interact with the virtual world and other avatars in real time.

- **User-Generated Content**: Unlike traditional media, where content is largely controlled by centralized entities, the Metaverse is built on user-generated content. Users not only consume experiences but also create, build, and modify the virtual world around them. From creating 3D models, animations, and games to designing virtual items and environments, users play a significant role in shaping the Metaverse.

4.2 How the Metaverse Works

The Metaverse is not just one platform or application but a decentralized network of connected virtual worlds and experiences. Users can navigate through these spaces, building their presence and participating in diverse activities like socializing, gaming, attending concerts, working, and shopping. Here's how the Metaverse works from a technical perspective, focusing on key components like virtual real estate, avatars, and digital identity.

Virtual Real Estate

Virtual real estate is the land or space within a Metaverse environment where users can build or interact with other users. Just like physical real estate, virtual land can be bought, sold, developed, and even leased. In fact, virtual real estate has become one of the most lucrative areas of the Metaverse, with individuals and companies investing in prime virtual land for business, entertainment, and personal use.

The concept of virtual real estate is most clearly seen in platforms like **Decentraland**, **The Sandbox**, and **Somnium Space**, where users purchase land using cryptocurrency. In these virtual worlds, owners can design their own properties, build structures, host events, or create experiences that other users can interact with. As virtual real estate gains more popularity, we see more businesses setting up shop in these spaces, offering virtual goods and services to users.

These digital properties are typically purchased using cryptocurrency (commonly Ethereum) and are registered as NFTs (non-fungible tokens), ensuring ownership and scarcity. The NFT aspect allows virtual land to be tracked and transferred between users, with each piece of land being unique and verifiable.

Avatars and Digital Identity

In the Metaverse, users navigate the virtual worlds through avatars, which are digital representations of themselves. These avatars can be highly customizable, with users able to change their appearance, outfits, and accessories. The avatar serves as the user's identity within the virtual space, allowing them to interact with the environment and other users.

Avatars are more than just static figures—they are interactive, dynamic, and responsive. Advanced avatars can mimic real-world actions through motion capture technology, allowing users to express emotions, movements, and gestures, which further enhance social interactions. Moreover, avatars can evolve over time as users accumulate virtual assets, change their appearance, or participate in different experiences.

As users spend more time in the Metaverse, avatars become a key component of their digital identity. This identity is fluid, allowing users to switch between different platforms or virtual worlds while maintaining a consistent presence across their virtual experiences. The ability to carry your avatar, digital assets, and personal history from one virtual space to another is a key part of the Metaverse's vision of interoperability.

Virtual Economy and Digital Assets

The Metaverse operates on its own virtual economy, where users can buy, sell, and trade digital goods and services. This economy is powered by virtual currencies, with **cryptocurrencies** like Ethereum and **centralized platforms** (like Facebook's Horizon Workrooms) each having their own digital currencies to facilitate transactions.

Digital assets in the Metaverse are often represented as NFTs. NFTs are unique tokens on the blockchain that represent ownership of digital goods, ranging from virtual real estate to in-game items, clothing, and even digital art. The value of NFTs is based on their uniqueness, scarcity, and demand. These assets can be bought, sold, or traded, and because they are stored on the blockchain, they provide verifiable ownership.

This digital economy extends to businesses, which are able to monetize their presence in the Metaverse by selling virtual goods, running advertisements, hosting events, or offering virtual services. For example, brands like **Nike** and **Gucci** have already begun to create digital versions of their products, selling them as NFTs in virtual worlds, while **artists** are creating virtual performances and digital art that can be collected as NFTs.

4.3 The Role of Blockchain in the Metaverse

Blockchain technology is the backbone of the Metaverse's economy and infrastructure. It ensures decentralization, transparency, and security, making the Metaverse an open and accessible space for anyone to participate in.

NFTs and Digital Ownership

Non-fungible tokens (NFTs) are digital representations of ownership of unique assets, and they play a pivotal role in the Metaverse. These tokens are stored on blockchain networks, ensuring that they are one-of-a-kind, traceable, and tamper-proof. NFTs enable users to own digital property, from virtual land to digital art and even in-game assets, such as skins, weapons, or clothing.

In the Metaverse, NFTs are used to represent ownership of virtual real estate, digital art, fashion items, and more. Ownership of NFTs can be transferred seamlessly between users and can be sold, rented, or gifted, making it easy to monetize digital assets.

The decentralized nature of blockchain ensures that these transactions are secure and transparent, as every action is recorded on a public ledger. This eliminates the need for intermediaries like banks or auction houses, creating a more direct and frictionless exchange of value.

Virtual Currencies and Smart Contracts

Alongside NFTs, virtual currencies like **Bitcoin** and **Ethereum** are essential for transacting in the Metaverse. These cryptocurrencies are used to buy virtual goods, purchase land, or participate in various virtual economies. Many Metaverse platforms have their own native tokens—such as **Mana** in Decentraland or **SAND** in The Sandbox—that can be used for in-platform transactions.

Smart contracts, which are self-executing contracts with the terms of the agreement directly written into code, are also crucial for the Metaverse. Smart contracts allow for secure, automated transactions without the need for third-party validation. For example, smart contracts can be used to facilitate the sale of virtual land, ensuring that ownership is transferred once payment is made and that the transaction is verified on the blockchain.

Decentralization and Governance

Blockchain enables the Metaverse to function in a decentralized manner, removing the need for centralized control by a single entity. This decentralization ensures that users have more control over their digital experiences and assets, and it fosters a more open and inclusive environment.

Decentralized Autonomous Organizations (DAOs) are one example of governance in the Metaverse. DAOs allow users to vote on decisions related to the development and management of virtual worlds, giving the community a voice in shaping the direction of the Metaverse.

4.4 Real-World Applications of the Metaverse

The Metaverse is not just a futuristic concept—it is already being applied across a wide range of industries, from gaming and entertainment to education and commerce. Here's a closer look at how the Metaverse is being used in the real world:

1. Social Interaction

The Metaverse offers users the ability to socialize, meet new people, and participate in shared experiences. Platforms like **Horizon Worlds** by Facebook (now Meta) and **AltspaceVR** enable people to interact with one another in a virtual space, where they can engage in conversations, attend virtual events, or simply hang out.

Virtual gatherings, such as virtual concerts or parties, are becoming increasingly popular. These events offer people a chance to experience live performances or social events in a fully immersive virtual space, bridging the gap between physical and digital interactions.

2. Gaming

Gaming is one of the most popular applications of the Metaverse. Platforms like **Roblox**, **Fortnite**, and **Minecraft** already offer virtual worlds where users can play games, socialize, and create content. These games have pioneered the concept of virtual economies, where users can buy, sell, and trade virtual items, such as skins, avatars, and in-game assets.

The Metaverse extends this concept further, offering larger, more immersive worlds where players can create their own adventures, explore, and engage with other users in a shared experience.

3. Work and Collaboration

The Metaverse is also transforming the way we work. Virtual offices, meeting rooms, and collaborative spaces are increasingly being built in the Metaverse, providing a more interactive alternative to traditional video conferencing tools like Zoom.

Companies like **Spatial** and **Microsoft** are already developing Metaverse platforms for virtual meetings, where employees can collaborate, share ideas, and interact with 3D models and virtual whiteboards in a way that feels more engaging than the typical video call.

4. Commerce

The Metaverse is opening up new frontiers in commerce, particularly in the form of virtual retail. Digital stores, virtual marketplaces, and NFT-based products are allowing brands and entrepreneurs to tap into a global virtual economy. Brands like **Nike** and **Gucci** are already creating and selling digital fashion, while virtual marketplaces such as **Decentraland** and **The Sandbox** are thriving as hubs for virtual real estate and digital goods.

4.5 Hands-On Project: Building a Virtual Space

In this hands-on project, we will walk through the process of creating a simple Metaverse-style environment using Unity, a popular game development platform. This project will introduce you to the foundational concepts of creating 3D spaces and interacting with the Metaverse.

Step 1: Setting Up Unity for VR Development

1. **Install Unity**:
   Begin by downloading and installing **Unity Hub** from the official Unity website. Once installed, open Unity Hub and create a new 3D project.

2. **Install AR/VR SDKs**:
   Depending on your platform, install the necessary SDKs for VR (like **Oculus SDK** for Unity or **SteamVR**) to enable immersive interaction in your virtual space.

Step 2: Building Your Virtual Space

1. **Create the Environment**:
   Start by building the basic layout of your virtual world. Add objects like terrain, walls, furniture, and lighting. Unity provides various 3D assets you can use for free or purchase from the Unity Asset Store.

2. **Add Interactivity**:
   Implement basic interactions such as object picking or movement using Unity's scripting tools. For example, using the C# programming language, you can create a script that allows

users to interact with virtual objects, changing their state when clicked or touched.

Step 3: Testing the Virtual Environment

1. **Deploy to VR Headset**:

   Once you've set up the basic environment, deploy it to your VR headset or desktop to test the navigation, interactions, and overall experience. Ensure that everything works as expected and make adjustments where needed.

Chapter 5: NFTs and the Digital Economy

5.1 What Are NFTs?

Non-fungible tokens (NFTs) are revolutionizing the concept of ownership in the digital realm. To fully understand NFTs, it's crucial to break down the term "non-fungible" and explore their underlying technology and functionality.

Non-Fungible Tokens Explained

At a basic level, a **token** is a digital representation of something—whether it's an item, asset, or currency. A token can be fungible or non-fungible:

- **Fungible tokens** are interchangeable with one another. This means that each unit of the token has the same value. Cryptocurrencies like **Bitcoin** or **Ethereum** are prime examples. One

Bitcoin is always equivalent to another, and each unit holds the same value.

- **Non-fungible tokens (NFTs),** on the other hand, are unique and not interchangeable. Each NFT has distinct properties and value, often linked to a digital asset such as art, music, videos, or virtual goods. No two NFTs are the same, and this uniqueness is what gives them their value.

NFTs are built on blockchain technology—typically **Ethereum**—which ensures their authenticity, provenance, and scarcity. Each NFT contains metadata and attributes that distinguish it from any other token, providing proof of ownership and a clear transaction history. This decentralized ledger prevents unauthorized copies or forgeries, making NFTs a revolutionary tool for verifying ownership in the digital world.

How NFTs Enable Digital Ownership

Before NFTs, digital content, such as images, videos, and music, existed in a unique, intangible form that was easily replicable. For example, a digital art piece could be copied countless times, making it difficult to assign ownership. NFTs resolve this issue by providing a secure and verifiable proof of ownership for digital assets.

When an artist creates an NFT, they encode the asset's unique identifier and relevant details into the blockchain, making it impossible to duplicate or alter. The owner of the NFT has rights to that specific asset, even if others can view or it. This creates a system of digital ownership akin to owning physical art or collectibles, but within the digital world.

NFTs work like certificates of authenticity. They establish digital ownership in a way that was previously not possible, ensuring that the owner has the exclusive rights to the asset. These tokens can be bought, sold, or traded in secondary markets, allowing artists and creators to benefit from resales through smart contracts, which automatically trigger royalty payments to the original creator each time the NFT changes hands.

In essence, NFTs introduce a whole new level of digital scarcity, granting verifiable ownership to the buyer while enabling creators to retain control over their work in the digital economy.

5.2 NFTs in Art, Music, and Entertainment

The emergence of NFTs has had a profound impact on creative industries like art, music, and entertainment, offering creators new opportunities for monetization and engagement with their audiences. NFTs allow digital creators to tokenize their works, sell them directly to consumers, and retain ownership rights that persist through secondary sales. This new paradigm has opened the door for creators to maintain more control over the value of their work.

The Explosion of NFTs in Creative Industries

The explosion of NFTs in creative sectors has taken the art world, in particular, by storm. Artists who previously struggled to profit from digital work have found a direct route to financial success through the sale of NFTs. Rather than relying on traditional galleries, digital platforms, or print editions, creators can now sell unique works of digital art directly to collectors, often for record-breaking sums.

This shift has given rise to a new generation of **NFT artists** who are reshaping the art market. Rather than simply selling physical paintings or prints, digital artists are creating animated works, interactive experiences, and generative art—pieces that live in the digital world, accessible to anyone with an internet connection.

NFT Art Platforms like **OpenSea**, **Rarible**, and **Foundation** have become popular marketplaces where artists can list their digital works as NFTs. These platforms allow buyers and sellers to engage in a transparent, peer-to-peer market, removing intermediaries and empowering both creators and collectors.

Famous NFT Success Stories

The meteoric rise of NFTs has led to several success stories that have captured the public's attention and elevated digital art to new heights:

- **Beeple's "Everydays: The First 5000 Days"**: Beeple, a digital artist known for creating daily digital art pieces for over a decade, became the first artist to sell a purely digital artwork as an NFT for **$69.3 million** at a Christie's auction. This sale marked a turning point for the art world, as it brought NFTs into the mainstream conversation, sparking widespread interest in digital art and NFTs.

- **CryptoPunks**:
  CryptoPunks, one of the earliest NFT projects created by **Larva Labs**, consists of 10,000 unique 24x24 pixel art characters, each with distinct features and attributes. Initially distributed for free in 2017, these tokens have skyrocketed in value, with some CryptoPunks selling for tens of millions of dollars. The project's success has cemented CryptoPunks as a symbol of the early NFT movement, turning them into digital collectibles with cultural significance.

- **Kings of Leon's NFT Album Release**:
  In 2021, the band **Kings of Leon** became the first major band to release an album as an NFT. Their album, *When You See Yourself*, was sold in various NFT formats, including exclusive content, digital artwork, and limited edition vinyl. This breakthrough signaled the potential of NFTs in the music industry, offering artists new ways to monetize their music while engaging with fans on a deeper level.

These success stories illustrate how NFTs have provided artists with new channels for revenue generation, enabling them to reach a global audience, control their digital assets, and benefit from resales through blockchain-powered royalties.

5.3 Real-World Use Cases of NFTs

Beyond the art world, NFTs are being integrated into numerous industries, unlocking new use cases and expanding the scope of what digital ownership can represent. From virtual goods to real estate, here are some of the key areas where NFTs are making an impact.

Virtual Goods

Virtual goods, including in-game items, skins, and collectibles, have been a mainstay in gaming for years. However, NFTs have taken this concept to the next level by enabling true ownership of digital assets. In-game items that are tokenized as NFTs can be bought, sold, and traded on secondary markets, empowering gamers to monetize their digital investments.

- **Axie Infinity**:
  In the blockchain-based game **Axie Infinity**, players collect, breed, and battle creatures

called Axies. These creatures are tokenized as NFTs, and players can trade them in the game's marketplace. The game has generated millions in revenue, with players earning real-world income through the sale of their NFTs.

- **Decentraland**:
  Decentraland is a virtual world where users can buy, sell, and trade virtual land as NFTs. This virtual land is used for building experiences such as art galleries, social spaces, and storefronts. NFTs in Decentraland represent the ownership of these virtual assets, allowing players to profit from their virtual property.

Real Estate

Virtual real estate is one of the most interesting and lucrative use cases for NFTs. Just like physical real estate, virtual properties within digital worlds can be bought, sold, or rented. These digital spaces are becoming increasingly valuable, with virtual land sales reaching tens of millions of dollars.

- **The Sandbox**:
  The Sandbox is a decentralized gaming platform where users can buy virtual land and create their own experiences. NFT-based land

ownership within The Sandbox enables players to develop games, host events, and monetize virtual properties. The platform's NFT marketplace facilitates the trade of these assets, which are represented by unique tokens on the blockchain.

Collectibles

NFTs have become a dominant force in the collectibles space, offering a digital alternative to physical collectibles such as trading cards, stamps, or memorabilia. These digital collectibles are verified on the blockchain, ensuring their rarity and authenticity.

- **NBA Top Shot**:
  NBA Top Shot allows basketball fans to collect, buy, and sell officially licensed NBA collectible highlights as NFTs. Each moment is tokenized as a unique NFT, and collectors can purchase or trade these digital assets. Top Shot has attracted millions of dollars in sales, further cementing NFTs as a legitimate form of digital collectibles.

- **CryptoKitties**:
  CryptoKitties was one of the first NFT-based

games to become widely popular, allowing players to collect, breed, and trade virtual cats. These cats are unique digital assets, and some have sold for hundreds of thousands of dollars. CryptoKitties helped establish NFTs as a viable method of creating digital scarcity in collectibles.

Fashion and Wearables

NFTs are also making waves in the fashion industry, allowing designers to tokenize virtual clothing and fashion items. These digital assets can be used to customize avatars, participate in virtual fashion shows, or even represent ownership of exclusive virtual items.

- **Rtfkt Studios**:
  Rtfkt Studios is a virtual fashion company that creates NFT-based sneakers and digital wearables. Their collaborations with prominent brands have driven the market for virtual fashion, with collectors purchasing limited-edition virtual items for their avatars and social media profiles.

5.4 Hands-On Project: Creating Your Own NFT Collection

In this hands-on project, we will guide you through the process of creating your own NFT collection. This step-by-step guide will introduce you to the process of minting and listing NFTs, allowing you to launch your own digital assets on a blockchain.

Step 1: Setting Up the Development Environment

Before you can create and mint NFTs, you need to set up a few tools and accounts:

1. **Install MetaMask**:
   MetaMask is a cryptocurrency wallet and gateway to the Ethereum blockchain. Install the MetaMask extension for your web browser and create a new wallet. Ensure that your MetaMask wallet has some Ethereum (ETH) for transaction fees (gas fees).

2. **Set Up an Ethereum Wallet**:
   If you don't already have an Ethereum wallet, you'll need to create one. Ethereum is the most widely used blockchain for NFTs, and you'll use it to interact with platforms like OpenSea. Use MetaMask to manage your wallet.

Step 2: Designing Your NFTs

Before minting your NFTs, you need to design your digital assets. These can range from 2D images to 3D models or even interactive art.

1. **Create Artwork**:
   Use software like **Adobe Photoshop**, **Illustrator**, or **Blender** to create your artwork. Each piece will be unique, so make sure to design assets that are visually appealing and aligned with your brand or concept.

2. **Save and Prepare Files**:
   Save your digital assets in formats such as **JPEG**, **PNG**, or **GIF** for 2D artwork, or **FBX** or **GLTF** for 3D models. Ensure the resolution is suitable for displaying online.

Step 3: Minting Your NFTs

1. **Upload Artwork to OpenSea**:
   OpenSea is one of the most popular NFT marketplaces. After setting up your wallet, log in to OpenSea and navigate to the "Create" section. Upload your digital files and fill in details like the name, description, and properties of your NFT.

2. **Mint the NFTs**:
   Once your artwork is uploaded, you can mint (or create) your NFT by paying a gas fee. This fee is required to write your NFT to the Ethereum blockchain. After minting, your NFT will be live and available for purchase or sale.

Step 4: Listing Your NFTs for Sale

1. **Set Pricing**:
   Once your NFT is minted, you can set your listing price. Decide whether you want to sell at a fixed price, auction, or through a reserve price. You can also offer special editions or rarity tiers to make your collection more appealing.

2. **Market Your Collection**:
   Share your collection on social media, NFT communities, and marketplaces to gain exposure. Platforms like **Twitter**, **Discord**, and **Instagram** have thriving NFT communities that can help promote your work.

Chapter 6: Web3 – The Decentralized Web

6.1 What Is Web3?

Web3, also known as the decentralized web, represents the next stage in the evolution of the internet. It builds on the foundations of the previous versions of the web—Web1 and Web2—while introducing key innovations that redefine how we interact with online content, services, and each other.

To understand Web3, it's important to first understand how the web has evolved over time. From the early days of the internet to today's dominant centralized platforms, Web3 promises to introduce a new level of control, ownership, and interoperability.

The Evolution from Web1 and Web2

1. **Web1 – The Static Web (Early 1990s to Early 2000s)**
   The internet began as Web1, a static web consisting primarily of one-way communication. Websites were simple, informational pages, where users could consume content but had little to no interaction or ability to contribute. Web1 was read-only, with content presented in HTML and hosted on centralized servers.

Example: Early websites like **AOL** or basic news sites represented the internet of Web1, where users could read information but not interact or contribute content.

2. **Web2 – The Social Web (Mid-2000s to Present)**
   The emergence of Web2 marked a significant shift from static content to dynamic, interactive platforms. The key innovation was the rise of user-generated content (UGC), social media, and collaboration platforms. Web2 gave rise to giants like **Facebook, YouTube, Twitter**, and **Amazon**, where users could create profiles,

post content, and interact with others in real time.

However, Web2 is also characterized by centralized control, where a small number of companies control user data, content, and interactions. These companies profit from user activity by collecting and monetizing personal data, which has raised concerns about privacy, surveillance, and monopolies.

Example: Platforms like **Instagram** and **YouTube** are Web2 applications. While they offer a rich interactive experience for users, the underlying data and content are controlled by centralized entities.

3. **Web3 – The Decentralized Web (Present and Future)**
   Web3 introduces the concept of decentralization, where power is distributed across many nodes, rather than being concentrated in the hands of a few corporations. It is powered by blockchain technology, which allows for trustless, peer-to-peer interactions without the need for intermediaries like banks, governments, or tech giants.

Web3 is about **ownership** and **control**. Users own their data, digital assets, and identities, and they participate in decentralized networks and communities. Instead of logging into platforms governed by centralized entities, users can interact directly with decentralized applications (DApps), and transactions can occur using cryptocurrencies without the need for traditional financial institutions.

Example: Decentralized finance (DeFi) protocols like **Uniswap** or **Compound** are Web3 applications, where users can exchange cryptocurrencies and earn interest without relying on centralized banks or financial institutions.

Web3 is also built on the idea of **interoperability**, where different applications and platforms work seamlessly together, and **permissionless** access, meaning anyone can participate in the network without needing approval from a central authority.

6.2 Key Principles of Web3

Web3 is defined by several key principles that distinguish it from previous versions of the web. These principles focus on decentralization, user empowerment, and transparency. Below, we dive into the core concepts that make Web3 unique.

Ownership, Privacy, and Data Control

One of the most significant changes that Web3 introduces is the **ownership** of data and digital assets. In the Web2 world, platforms like **Google**, **Facebook**, and **Amazon** own and control the vast amounts of personal data that users generate. This gives these platforms immense power, allowing them to monetize user activity and content, often without users' full awareness or consent.

In Web3, **users have control over their data**. By using decentralized technologies like **blockchain**, users can own their identities, data, and assets. Blockchain's immutable ledger ensures that once data is stored, it cannot be tampered with, and users have the ability to share or withhold their data as they see fit. This puts the power back into the hands of the user, allowing for greater privacy and autonomy online.

Furthermore, Web3 enables the creation of **self-sovereign identities** (SSIs), which allow users to control their online identity through cryptographic keys rather than relying on centralized entities for authentication. These SSIs ensure that users have full ownership over their identity without needing to trust external authorities.

Example: Projects like **Sovrin** and **uPort** are building decentralized identity systems that allow users to control their personal data across multiple platforms, enhancing privacy and security.

Cryptocurrencies, DAOs, and Smart Contracts

Web3 relies heavily on blockchain technology to create a decentralized economy. The key components of this decentralized economy are cryptocurrencies, **decentralized autonomous organizations (DAOs)**, and **smart contracts**.

1. **Cryptocurrencies**:
   Cryptocurrencies like **Bitcoin** and **Ethereum** are digital currencies that use cryptography to secure transactions and control the creation of new units. These cryptocurrencies are based on decentralized networks (blockchains) that allow for peer-to-peer transactions without the need for intermediaries like banks. In Web3, cryptocurrencies serve as the primary medium of exchange and store of value, allowing for seamless, borderless transactions.

Example: Ethereum is not only a cryptocurrency but also a platform for decentralized applications (DApps), powered by its native cryptocurrency, **Ether (ETH)**.

2. **DAOs (Decentralized Autonomous Organizations):**

   DAOs are organizations that operate on a blockchain and are governed by their members through smart contracts. These organizations have no central leadership, and decisions are made collectively by stakeholders who vote on proposals. DAOs enable truly decentralized governance, where participants can contribute to the decision-making process, ensuring that power is distributed across the network.

Example: MakerDAO is a DAO that governs the stablecoin **Dai**. The community of Dai holders can propose and vote on changes to the protocol, ensuring that the stablecoin remains decentralized and trustless.

3. **Smart Contracts:**

   Smart contracts are self-executing contracts with the terms directly written into lines of code. These contracts automatically execute when predefined conditions are met, removing the need for intermediaries or manual enforcement. Smart contracts are the backbone of Web3 applications, allowing for trustless transactions, automated processes, and decentralized applications (DApps).

Example: In the world of DeFi, **Uniswap** uses smart contracts to enable users to exchange cryptocurrencies directly, without the need for an intermediary exchange. Similarly, **Compound** uses smart contracts to facilitate lending and borrowing in a decentralized manner.

Decentralization and Trustless Interactions

Web3 is built on the principle of **decentralization**, meaning that control is distributed across a network rather than being held by a single entity. This decentralization is made possible through blockchain technology, where all participants have access to the same data and can verify transactions without needing to trust a central authority.

In Web3, **trustless interactions** become the norm. Trust is built into the system through cryptographic proofs and consensus mechanisms rather than relying on third parties. For example, blockchain uses

Proof of Work (PoW) or **Proof of Stake (PoS)** mechanisms to ensure the integrity of transactions and the security of the network, without relying on centralized validators.

6.3 Web3 in Practice

Web3 isn't just a theoretical concept—it is already being applied in various industries, from finance and art to entertainment and governance. Below are some of the most impactful applications of Web3.

Applications in Finance (DeFi)

Decentralized Finance (DeFi) is one of the most prominent and transformative use cases of Web3. DeFi aims to recreate traditional financial systems—such as lending, borrowing, trading, and insurance—using decentralized technologies like blockchain and smart contracts. By removing intermediaries like banks, DeFi platforms offer more transparent, accessible, and efficient financial services.

- **Lending and Borrowing**:
  Platforms like **Aave** and **Compound** allow users to lend and borrow cryptocurrencies without relying on traditional banks. These platforms

use smart contracts to automate lending agreements, determine interest rates, and manage collateral, all while maintaining transparency and security.

- **Decentralized Exchanges (DEXs)**: Decentralized exchanges like **Uniswap** and **SushiSwap** enable users to trade cryptocurrencies directly with one another, without the need for an intermediary exchange. These platforms rely on smart contracts to facilitate trades and provide liquidity, and they allow users to retain full control over their funds.

- **Stablecoins**: Stablecoins like **Dai** and **USDC** are cryptocurrencies pegged to a stable asset, such as the US dollar, to reduce volatility. These coins are widely used in the DeFi ecosystem as a stable medium of exchange or collateral.

Applications in Art (NFTs)

Web3 has fundamentally changed the way digital art is created, bought, and sold, thanks to the introduction of **non-fungible tokens (NFTs)**. NFTs allow digital creators to tokenize their art, proving its authenticity, ownership, and scarcity.

- **NFT Marketplaces**:
  Platforms like **OpenSea**, **Rarible**, and **Foundation** allow artists to mint, list, and sell their NFTs, creating a global marketplace for digital art. These marketplaces leverage Web3 technology to ensure the provenance and ownership of each artwork, enabling artists to monetize their work and retain control over their creations.

- **NFT Royalties**:
  One of the revolutionary aspects of NFTs is the ability for artists to receive royalties from secondary sales. Smart contracts ensure that a percentage of each resale is automatically sent back to the original creator, providing an ongoing revenue stream that wasn't possible in the traditional art market.

Web3 in Governance and Social Networks

Web3 is also transforming governance and social networks by enabling decentralized, user-governed platforms. This gives users more control over their data, content, and interactions online.

- **Decentralized Social Networks**:
  Platforms like **Mastodon** and **Steemit** are
  decentralized alternatives to traditional social
  media platforms like Twitter and Facebook. In
  these decentralized networks, users control
  their data and are often rewarded for creating
  content through cryptocurrency.

- **Decentralized Governance**:
  DAOs (Decentralized Autonomous
  Organizations) are being used to govern
  everything from virtual worlds and financial
  protocols to communities and open-source
  projects. DAOs allow stakeholders to vote on
  proposals and make decisions collectively,
  ensuring a democratic and transparent
  governance structure.

6.4 Hands-On Project: Building a Simple DApp

In this hands-on project, we will guide you through
building a simple **Decentralized Application (DApp)**
on the **Ethereum blockchain** using **smart contracts**.
By the end of this project, you will understand the

basics of how DApps function and how smart contracts are deployed to the Ethereum network.

Step 1: Setting Up Your Development Environment

1. **Install Node.js**:
   Download and install **Node.js**, which will allow you to run JavaScript code outside the browser. You can download it from the official website.

2. **Install Truffle Suite**:
   Truffle is a development framework for Ethereum that simplifies smart contract deployment and testing. Install Truffle using the following command:

bash

npm install -g truffle

3. **Install Ganache**:
   Ganache is a personal blockchain for Ethereum development. It allows you to test your smart contracts in a local environment before deploying them to the Ethereum network. Download Ganache from the Truffle website.

4. **Set Up MetaMask:**
   MetaMask is a browser extension that allows you to interact with the Ethereum blockchain. Set up a MetaMask wallet and connect it to your local Ganache blockchain.

Step 2: Writing Your Smart Contract

1. **Create a New Truffle Project:**
   Use Truffle to create a new project by running the following command:

bash

```
truffle init
```

2. **Write a Simple Smart Contract:**
   Create a new file in the contracts directory called SimpleStorage.sol. This contract will allow users to store a number on the blockchain.

solidity

```
pragma solidity ^0.8.0;
```

```solidity
contract SimpleStorage {

    uint256 storedData;


    function set(uint256 x) public {

        storedData = x;

    }


    function get() public view returns (uint256) {

        return storedData;

    }

}
```

Step 3: Deploying the Smart Contract

1. **Compile the Smart Contract**:
   Run the following command to compile your smart contract:

```bash
bash
```

```
truffle compile
```

2. **Deploy the Smart Contract to Ganache**:
   Create a migration file in the migrations folder
   to deploy your smart contract. Then, run:

bash

truffle migrate

Step 4: Building the Frontend DApp

1. **Set Up Web3.js**:
   Web3.js is a JavaScript library that allows you to
   interact with the Ethereum blockchain from the
   frontend. Install it via npm:

bash

npm install web3

2. **Connect the Frontend to MetaMask**:
   Use Web3.js to connect your DApp to
   MetaMask and interact with the deployed smart
   contract. Display the stored value and provide a
   button to set a new value.

Chapter 7: Integrating AR and VR into Industries

7.1 The Role of Immersive Tech in Healthcare

Immersive technologies such as Augmented Reality (AR) and Virtual Reality (VR) have rapidly gained traction in the healthcare industry, transforming everything from medical training and patient care to surgery and rehabilitation. These technologies are enabling healthcare professionals to provide better, more precise care, while enhancing the patient experience. In this section, we will explore the various ways AR and VR are reshaping healthcare and look at some of the most promising applications in the field.

Virtual Training and Medical Simulations

One of the most significant advancements in healthcare driven by AR and VR is in **medical training and simulations**. These technologies allow healthcare professionals to practice and refine their skills in a controlled, virtual environment, reducing the risk of human error during real-world procedures.

1. **Surgical Training**:
   Surgery requires an immense amount of precision, skill, and practice. Traditionally, surgical trainees had to rely on cadavers or live patients to gain hands-on experience, often under tight supervision. With VR and AR, medical professionals can now practice surgeries in a virtual environment where they can simulate complex procedures without any risk to the patient.

Example: Programs like **Osso VR** and **Touch Surgery** use VR simulations to help medical students and surgeons practice surgeries. These simulations replicate real-life procedures, allowing users to engage in a fully immersive experience that enhances their technical skills and clinical decision-making. The interactive nature of these simulations also provides instant feedback, which is invaluable for learning.

2. **Anatomy Learning**:
   AR and VR are also transforming the way medical students learn about human anatomy. Virtual cadavers and 3D models allow students to explore the body's systems in a highly interactive and visual way, enabling them to gain a deeper understanding of complex structures. AR can be used to overlay digital anatomy models onto a real body, helping students see organs and systems in real time.

Example: ZSpace offers an interactive 3D visualization tool that enables medical students to interact with 3D models of the human body. Through AR and VR, students can examine organs, tissues, and muscles in ways that would be impossible with traditional methods.

3. **Emergency Response Training**:
   VR-based emergency response training programs are used to simulate real-world medical emergencies, such as cardiac arrest, trauma injuries, and complicated childbirth scenarios. These simulations allow healthcare

workers to practice life-saving techniques without putting patients at risk. The training scenarios are designed to be highly immersive, challenging trainees to make quick, critical decisions in real time.

Example: VRpatients is a VR training solution that offers medical emergency simulations to help healthcare professionals practice handling life-threatening conditions, improving their readiness and response times.

Medical Simulations for Diagnosis and Treatment

1. **Surgical Planning and Visualization**:
   AR is helping surgeons plan complex operations by overlaying digital images or scans onto a patient's body. This allows doctors to visualize the exact location of tumors, organs, and blood vessels, ensuring that they can make more accurate decisions during surgery. With AR, surgeons can access crucial data without needing to take their eyes off the patient, enhancing both precision and efficiency.

Example: Microsoft HoloLens is used by medical professionals to view 3D scans of a patient's body during surgery. The holographic data overlays the patient's body, allowing surgeons to plan their procedures in real-time and visualize complex structures from multiple angles.

2. **Pain Management**:
   Virtual reality has also found applications in managing and treating chronic pain. Studies have shown that VR can be used as an effective tool in distracting patients from pain during medical procedures or rehabilitation. VR environments provide immersive experiences that can relax patients and reduce their perception of pain.

Example: **Cool!**, a VR platform developed by Cedars-Sinai, uses immersive experiences to help patients undergoing painful procedures such as burn wound dressing changes. The platform immerses patients in calming, soothing environments, offering distraction from the discomfort of the procedure.

Patient Care and Therapy

1. **Mental Health Treatment**:
   VR and AR are increasingly being used to treat mental health conditions like PTSD, anxiety, and phobias. VR exposure therapy helps patients

confront their fears in a safe, controlled environment, where they can gradually desensitize themselves to the objects or situations they fear.

Example: Bravemind, developed by the University of Southern California, is a VR system used for PTSD treatment. It immerses veterans in virtual simulations of warzone environments, allowing them to re-live traumatic experiences under the supervision of a therapist, helping them process and overcome their trauma.

2. **Physical Rehabilitation**:
   VR is also revolutionizing physical rehabilitation by offering patients engaging, interactive exercises. These therapies are designed to make physical rehabilitation more fun and motivating, which can lead to improved outcomes. Patients can perform physical exercises in a virtual environment, with feedback provided on their movements and progress.

Example: Rehab-Robotics offers VR-based rehabilitation devices that help patients recover from neurological conditions like stroke. These devices use virtual games and simulations to help patients regain motor skills, offering real-time feedback on their progress.

7.2 Immersive Technologies in Education

Education has always been a driving force behind the adoption of new technologies, and immersive technologies like AR and VR are no exception. In the classroom, these technologies provide opportunities for interactive, engaging, and hands-on learning, transforming how students learn and how educators teach.

Virtual Classrooms and Distance Learning

1. **Immersive Virtual Classrooms**:
   Traditional classrooms are increasingly being supplemented by immersive virtual classrooms, where students can interact with their teachers and classmates in real time in a fully immersive, 3D environment. These virtual classrooms replicate the dynamics of a physical classroom, but they allow students to be anywhere in the world while still

participating in discussions, lectures, and group activities.

Example: Engage is a VR platform that allows schools and universities to create virtual campuses, where students can attend classes, collaborate with peers, and engage with teachers in an immersive setting. This solution is particularly valuable for distance learning and international education programs, enabling real-time interaction from any location.

2. **Interactive Learning Environments**:
   AR and VR provide powerful tools for creating interactive and immersive learning experiences. For example, students can take virtual field trips to historical landmarks, museums, or even outer space. This hands-on approach to learning engages students in a way that textbooks or videos cannot, enhancing their understanding and retention of complex subjects.

Example: Google Expeditions offers virtual reality field trips to over 900 locations around the world, including the Great Wall of China, the surface of Mars, and the Galápagos Islands. Students can explore these locations in VR, gaining insights they wouldn't typically get in a traditional classroom setting.

1. **Simulations for Scientific Learning**:
   AR and VR can also be used to simulate complex scientific concepts, allowing students to interact with elements that are too small, too distant, or too dangerous to explore in a real-world setting. For example, students can visualize molecular structures in 3D, or conduct virtual chemical experiments that would be hazardous or impractical in a physical lab.

Example: **Labster** offers virtual science labs where students can experiment with complex lab equipment and conduct experiments without the need for a physical laboratory. These VR simulations provide a safe, cost-effective, and scalable way to deliver high-quality scientific education.

2. **Medical and Engineering Training**:
   In technical fields like medicine, engineering, and aviation, VR and AR are being used to simulate complex tasks that students would traditionally learn through hands-on training. These simulations allow for realistic, repeatable

practice, enabling students to develop critical skills in a low-risk environment.

Example: **Immersive Labs** offers a range of simulations that teach cybersecurity skills through interactive, immersive environments. Students can practice responding to real-world cyberattacks in a safe, controlled space, gaining experience without the consequences of real-world breaches.

7.3 AR and VR in Retail and Customer Experience

Immersive technologies like AR and VR are having a transformative impact on the retail sector, providing customers with innovative shopping experiences that bridge the gap between physical and digital worlds. These technologies enable brands to engage with customers in novel ways, creating experiences that are both interactive and memorable.

Virtual Try-Ons and Fitting Rooms

1. **Virtual Clothing Try-Ons**:
   AR is transforming the way people shop for clothing and accessories. Through virtual fitting rooms, customers can try on clothes virtually using their smartphone or smart mirror, without

needing to step into a store. This eliminates sizing issues and enhances the online shopping experience by allowing customers to see how clothing fits and looks in real time.

Example: Zara has implemented AR technology in their stores, allowing customers to try on outfits virtually using interactive mirrors. Shoppers can select clothing items from the store's rack, and the AR system will superimpose the clothing onto their reflection, giving them a sense of how the item will look before trying it on.

2. **Virtual Makeup Try-Ons**:
   Similarly, the beauty industry has embraced AR to enable customers to try on makeup virtually. By using the front camera of a smartphone or an in-store smart mirror, customers can see how different products—such as lipstick, foundation, or eyeshadow—will look on their skin tone, allowing them to make more informed purchase decisions.

Example: Sephora uses AR technology in its **Virtual Artist** tool, allowing customers to try on makeup products virtually. Customers can experiment with different shades and products in real-time, enhancing the shopping experience by offering personalized recommendations based on their facial features.

Interactive Shopping and Digital Showrooms

1. **Immersive Shopping Experiences**:
   VR allows retailers to create immersive shopping environments where customers can browse virtual stores from the comfort of their own homes. In these virtual stores, customers can pick out items, interact with products, and even experience the layout of the store in 3D, creating an engaging and unique shopping experience.

Example: IKEA Place is an app that uses AR to help customers visualize how furniture will look in their home before making a purchase. Users can place 3D models of furniture into their real-world living spaces using their smartphones, making it easier to select the right pieces without leaving their homes.

2. **Digital Showrooms**:
   Brands are also creating digital showrooms that allow customers to explore and interact with their products in 3D. Whether it's for cars, furniture, or luxury goods, these digital showrooms offer customers a way to see

products from all angles and even experience them in virtual environments.

Example: **Audius** is a company that allows customers to take virtual test drives of cars using VR. Prospective buyers can virtually experience the car's interior, exterior, and performance, all from the comfort of their homes.

7.4 Hands-On Project: Creating an AR/VR Experience for Retail

In this section, we will create a simple AR/VR shopping experience using Unity and the Oculus Rift. This hands-on project will give you an introduction to developing immersive retail experiences that you can customize to suit different products and retail environments.

Step 1: Setting Up the Development Environment

1. **Install Unity**:
   Download and install **Unity**, which will be the primary development environment for creating your AR/VR experience.

2. **Install Oculus SDK**:
   If you're using the Oculus Rift or Oculus Quest, download and install the **Oculus SDK** for Unity. This SDK provides the necessary tools for integrating Oculus VR hardware into your Unity projects.

Step 2: Building the Virtual Store Environment

1. **Create a 3D Environment**:
   Start by creating a simple 3D environment in Unity. This will serve as your virtual store or showroom. You can use Unity's built-in assets or import custom 3D models from the **Unity Asset Store** or programs like **Blender**.

2. **Add Interactive Objects**:
   Add interactive objects to your virtual store environment. These objects could represent items that customers can "pick up" and inspect, such as clothing, shoes, or electronics. Use Unity's physics and interaction systems to allow users to interact with these objects.

Step 3: Implementing AR or VR Functionality

1. **For VR**:
   If you're using VR, configure your Unity project

for VR compatibility by setting up the necessary Oculus SDK components. Implement user navigation, so customers can walk around the virtual store using the VR headset and controllers.

2. **For AR**:
   For AR, use **ARFoundation** in Unity, which allows you to deploy your app on both iOS and Android devices. Configure AR tracking to allow the app to place virtual items in the user's environment, giving the experience of interacting with products in a real-world context.

Step 4: Testing and Deployment

1. **Test the Experience**:
   Test the AR/VR experience to ensure everything works smoothly. Make sure that interactions are intuitive, and that users can easily navigate the store or try on virtual items.

2. **Deploy the Experience**:
   Deploy the experience to a VR headset like the **Oculus Rift** or **Oculus Quest** for VR, or to a smartphone for AR. Once the experience is set

up, users can interact with the digital store, trying on products, interacting with items, and making purchasing decisions.

Chapter 8: Challenges and Limitations of Immersive Technologies

8.1 Technical Challenges

Immersive technologies such as **Virtual Reality (VR)**, **Augmented Reality (AR)**, and **Mixed Reality (MR)** have transformed industries by providing engaging, interactive experiences that blur the line between the digital and physical worlds. However, despite their immense potential, these technologies still face several significant technical challenges that limit their widespread adoption and usage. In this section, we will explore key technical hurdles in immersive technology development, including hardware limitations, device requirements, latency, frame rates, and rendering issues.

Hardware Limitations and Device Requirements

One of the most significant barriers to the mainstream adoption of immersive technologies is the reliance on specialized, high-performance hardware. VR and AR applications require powerful processing power, precise tracking, and high-quality rendering to ensure a smooth and immersive experience. However, current devices often face significant constraints in terms of processing capacity, portability, and cost.

1. **Processing Power and Graphics Performance**:
   Immersive technologies demand substantial computational resources, particularly when rendering high-fidelity 3D environments in real-time. Virtual reality headsets, such as the **Oculus Rift** and **HTC Vive**, require powerful **Graphics Processing Units (GPUs)** and **Central Processing Units (CPUs)** to run simulations, render detailed environments, and track user interactions. These devices place a heavy demand on computational resources,

often requiring high-end gaming PCs or dedicated hardware to maintain consistent performance.

- **Standalone VR Devices**: Standalone VR headsets like the **Oculus Quest 2** have made significant strides in offering untethered, all-in-one VR experiences. However, these devices still face limitations in terms of processing power, as they rely on mobile-grade GPUs and processors to perform tasks that would typically require a more powerful, external PC. While these devices are lightweight and portable, the trade-off comes in the form of reduced graphical fidelity and performance.

- **Mobile AR Devices**: AR applications that run on smartphones or tablets face similar limitations. Although devices like **Apple's iPhone** and **Microsoft's HoloLens** have improved the AR experience, they are still limited by the mobile processors and battery life of the devices. Running AR applications with high computational demands can cause overheating, lag, or battery drain, making extended use less practical.

2. **Weight, Comfort, and Form Factor**:
   The physical design of immersive hardware is another challenge. VR headsets, in particular, often suffer from ergonomics issues such as weight and discomfort, especially during extended use. The bulkiness of traditional VR headsets can lead to neck strain, sweating, and discomfort. While some newer headsets have reduced weight and improved comfort, they still represent a barrier for casual users who may not want to wear bulky hardware.

AR devices such as smart glasses are also hindered by form factor limitations. Current AR glasses, such as **Microsoft HoloLens** or **Magic Leap**, are often too large and uncomfortable for extended wear. The challenge lies in creating lightweight, stylish, and comfortable wearables that can run AR applications seamlessly without requiring significant trade-offs in terms of performance or battery life.

3. **Battery Life and Power Constraints**:
   Both VR and AR applications demand high

energy consumption to power displays, sensors, tracking systems, and processors. VR headsets, especially mobile and standalone models, often experience significant battery drain during prolonged use. Users may find themselves needing to recharge their device frequently, which limits the device's usability for long sessions. Similarly, AR devices that rely on mobile devices for processing and display are limited by battery life, making them less viable for extended usage in real-world scenarios.

The need for high energy consumption in immersive technologies has spurred the development of new, more efficient hardware, but significant improvements in battery life are still needed before these technologies can become more accessible and convenient for consumers.

Latency, Frame Rates, and Rendering Issues

The success of immersive technologies hinges on the ability to render high-quality content with minimal latency and optimal frame rates. Latency, frame rates, and rendering are all critical factors in delivering a seamless, immersive experience. Any lag, stuttering, or visual artifacts can disrupt the user's sense of immersion, leading to motion sickness, discomfort, or a breakdown in the experience.

1. **Latency**:
   Latency refers to the time delay between a user's action (e.g., moving their head, reaching for an object, or making a gesture) and the system's response. In VR and AR, high latency can lead to discomfort and even motion sickness. In VR, when a user's head movement is not reflected accurately in the virtual environment in real-time, it can result in a disorienting experience, making the user feel disconnected from the digital world. Similarly, in AR, high latency can cause digital objects to lag behind real-world movements, making them appear disconnected or inaccurate.

   o **Ideal Latency Thresholds**: In VR, the ideal latency is **under 20 milliseconds**. Anything above this threshold may lead to discomfort and motion sickness. Reducing latency requires efficient processing, optimized network communication, and high-speed sensors to track user movements with minimal delay.

2. **Frame Rates**:

   Frame rates are another crucial aspect of immersive technology performance. VR and AR applications require high frame rates to maintain fluid, responsive interactions. In VR, frame rates of **90 Hz or higher** are considered the minimum standard for a smooth experience, while lower frame rates can lead to stutter, ghosting, or blurred visuals, disrupting the immersion. Similarly, AR applications rely on a stable frame rate to render virtual objects in sync with real-world environments. Inadequate frame rates can result in digital objects appearing jittery, out of sync, or poorly integrated into the physical world.

   - **Dynamic Frame Rates**: Achieving consistently high frame rates can be difficult due to the rendering demands of immersive environments. Optimizing the frame rate requires balancing graphical fidelity and performance, often through techniques such as **dynamic resolution scaling** or **spatial downsampling**.

3. **Rendering Issues**:

   Rendering is the process of generating the visual content that makes up the virtual environment. In VR, rendering must occur in real-time, as the user's movements dictate the changes in perspective and interaction. The rendering process for VR is particularly challenging because the system must produce two images—one for each eye—to create a stereoscopic 3D effect. Additionally, VR applications must account for rapid head movements and maintain a high frame rate, which can strain hardware and impact visual quality.

   - **Optimizing Rendering**: Techniques such as **foveated rendering** (where only the area in the user's direct line of sight is rendered in high detail) and **multi-view rendering** can help reduce the computational load and increase performance, allowing for better visuals and higher frame rates without overburdening hardware.

8.2 User Experience (UX) Challenges

Creating effective and engaging user experiences in immersive environments is no simple task. The user experience (UX) in AR, VR, and MR applications involves many factors, from designing intuitive controls to ensuring accessibility and comfort for a wide range of users. These challenges require careful consideration and a deep understanding of human behavior and interaction.

Creating Intuitive, Accessible Immersive Experiences

1. **User Interface (UI) Design**:
   Traditional **user interfaces** like menus, buttons, and text boxes do not translate well into VR and AR environments. In immersive environments, the UI must be intuitive and responsive to the user's movements, gaze, or gestures. Designing **spatial user interfaces** in which virtual elements are anchored in the 3D environment requires careful thought. Users should be able

to interact with virtual objects and controls in a way that feels natural and doesn't break the immersion.

- ○ **In VR**: UI elements are typically 3D objects that exist in the virtual space. Designers must create interfaces that are easy to access and interact with, often involving gesture controls or the use of VR controllers. UI elements should be placed within the user's reach, and menus should be organized in a way that does not overwhelm the user.

- ○ **In AR**: UI elements need to be integrated with the real world seamlessly. Overlays must be easy to read, and objects should be anchored to the real world in a way that feels natural. UI design in AR needs to ensure that digital content doesn't obscure important real-world information.

2. **Accessibility**:
Making immersive technologies accessible to a wide range of users is a significant challenge. People with different abilities should be able to

interact with immersive environments without experiencing discomfort or exclusion. Designing for accessibility means considering issues like **motion sickness**, **visual impairments**, and **limited mobility**.

- o **Motion Sickness**: VR motion sickness is one of the most common complaints from users, often caused by a mismatch between the user's physical movement and the movement of the virtual world. Designers can reduce the risk of motion sickness by implementing features like **snap-turning**, **reduced movement speed**, and **shorter session lengths**.

- o **Visual Accessibility**: AR and VR applications need to be designed with color blindness, contrast sensitivity, and other visual impairments in mind. Ensuring that interfaces are readable and providing options for text scaling, color adjustments, or audio descriptions can help make immersive experiences more accessible.

3. **Immersion and Engagement**:
   The ultimate goal of immersive technologies is to create a sense of presence, where users feel as though they are physically immersed in a virtual or augmented world. Achieving this level of immersion requires attention to detail in the user interface, environmental design, and interactivity. Failure to create a coherent, engaging experience can cause users to disconnect from the experience, resulting in frustration or disengagement.

   o **Example**: In VR gaming, failure to match the user's head movements

with corresponding changes in the virtual environment (e.g., not updating the scene quickly enough when the player turns their head) can break the feeling of immersion and cause discomfort.

8.3 Scalability and Performance Issues

As immersive technologies continue to grow in popularity, scalability becomes a key concern. The ability to deliver high-quality immersive experiences to a large audience, without sacrificing performance, is essential for the widespread adoption of these technologies. In this section, we will explore scalability issues and how they impact both VR and AR applications.

Blockchain Scaling and VR Hardware Constraints

1. **Blockchain Scaling**:
   Web3 technologies, particularly blockchain, present scalability challenges that need to be addressed for large-scale applications. **Smart contracts, NFTs**, and **decentralized applications (DApps)** require high transaction throughput, but the limitations of blockchain networks like **Ethereum**—including high fees and slow transaction speeds—present significant hurdles. As the Metaverse and other virtual economies grow, the ability to scale blockchain solutions is crucial.

   - **Solutions**: The development of **Layer 2** solutions, such as **Polygon** and **Optimism,** aims to solve scalability issues by processing transactions off-chain and only submitting final results to the main blockchain, reducing costs and improving transaction speed.

2. **VR Hardware Constraints**:
   The performance of VR applications is limited by the capabilities of hardware. The need for high-quality graphics, low latency, and smooth interactions creates a heavy computational burden on VR systems. While standalone VR devices are becoming more powerful, there are still significant constraints when it comes to rendering detailed environments at high frame rates.

   - **Optimization**: Developers are using techniques such as **foveated rendering**, **multi-resolution rendering**, and **dynamic resolution scaling** to reduce the computational load on VR systems while maintaining high-quality visuals.

8.4 Ethical and Privacy Concerns

With the increasing use of immersive technologies, ethical and privacy concerns are at the forefront of discussions. These technologies collect vast amounts of data, ranging from user movements to sensitive biometric information. How this data is collected, stored, and used is a critical issue that developers and regulators need to address.

Data Security, Surveillance, and Virtual Spaces

1. **Data Security**:
   Immersive technologies often collect highly personal data, including users' physical movements, biometric data (such as heart rate or eye tracking), and location data. Ensuring that this data is securely stored and transmitted is paramount to protecting user privacy. Without proper security measures, immersive platforms could become targets for data breaches or misuse.

2. **Surveillance**:
   Immersive technologies like AR glasses or VR headsets collect a wealth of data on users' activities, movements, and interactions. This data could potentially be used for surveillance purposes, raising concerns about privacy and personal autonomy. As these technologies become more widespread, there is a growing need for clear regulations on how this data is used and who has access to it.

3. **Ethical Concerns in Virtual Spaces**:
   As virtual spaces become more immersive and realistic, ethical concerns surrounding content moderation, harassment, and user safety will become increasingly important. Just as with social media platforms, developers of immersive environments must find ways to prevent abuse and ensure that users can interact in a safe and respectful manner.

8.5 Hands-On Project: Optimizing VR Performance

In this hands-on section, we will dive into practical steps for optimizing VR performance to ensure smooth and immersive experiences. By following these steps, you can enhance the performance of your VR applications, reducing latency, improving frame rates, and optimizing rendering to deliver a seamless experience.

1. **Frame Rate Monitoring and Testing**:
   - Begin by using the **Unity Profiler** or **Unreal Engine's built-in profiler** to monitor the frame rate and CPU/GPU

utilization. Aim for a target of **90 FPS** for VR applications.

2. **Optimizing Assets**:

   o Reduce polygon counts on 3D models by implementing **Level of Detail (LOD)** techniques, which dynamically adjust the complexity of objects based on their distance from the camera.

   o Compress textures and use **mipmaps** to reduce texture memory usage while maintaining high-quality visuals.

3. **Foveated Rendering**:

   o Implement **foveated rendering** to optimize the rendering workload by reducing the detail in the peripheral vision while maintaining high resolution in the user's central view. This significantly improves performance without sacrificing visual quality.

4. **Optimize Latency**:

   o Ensure that **motion tracking** is optimized by calibrating sensors and minimizing the time it takes for movement data to be processed and reflected in the VR environment. Implement techniques such as **prediction and smoothing** to reduce lag.

5. **Test Across Devices:**

   o Test the application on multiple VR headsets, including both high-end (e.g., Oculus Rift) and standalone (e.g., Oculus Quest) devices, to ensure consistent performance across various hardware configurations.

Chapter 9: The Future of AR, VR, and the Metaverse

9.1 Emerging Trends in Immersive Tech

Immersive technologies like Augmented Reality (AR), Virtual Reality (VR), and the Metaverse have already shown significant potential to transform industries such as healthcare, education, gaming, and entertainment. As we look towards the future, these technologies are evolving rapidly, with several emerging trends that promise to push the boundaries of what's possible. The integration of **artificial intelligence (AI)**, **mixed reality (MR)**, and the further development of virtual environments will redefine how users interact with digital worlds and physical spaces.

AI-Driven Experiences

One of the most exciting trends in immersive tech is the integration of **artificial intelligence** into AR and VR. AI has the potential to enhance these immersive experiences by providing more intelligent and dynamic interactions, improving user immersion, and personalizing experiences. AI-driven environments can adapt to a user's behavior, making each interaction more intuitive and responsive.

1. **AI in Virtual Worlds**:
   In the context of the Metaverse and virtual environments, AI can enable the creation of more realistic, interactive, and personalized worlds. Non-playable characters (NPCs) in VR games or virtual spaces can evolve based on AI algorithms, learning from users' actions and preferences. Rather than relying on pre-programmed scripts, AI-driven NPCs will behave and react more naturally, creating a more engaging and lifelike experience.

Example: AI in VR gaming is already enhancing player experiences. In games like **Red Dead Redemption 2**, AI-powered NPCs respond dynamically to player actions, creating a more immersive world. This type of

AI application can be expanded to the Metaverse, where users interact with both AI-driven avatars and human participants in a shared, evolving environment.

2. **Personalized Immersive Experiences**:
   AI can also use data from users to tailor experiences to individual preferences. By analyzing a user's behavior, preferences, and actions, immersive environments can adjust in real time. For example, in an AR shopping app, AI could recommend items based on a user's past interactions or even recognize their facial expressions and offer personalized content or suggestions.

Example: In **AI-powered VR therapy** applications, AI can help adjust the difficulty level of exercises or treatments based on the patient's progress. It can also analyze responses in real-time, providing feedback and modifying scenarios to keep the patient engaged and motivated.

3. **Natural Language Processing (NLP)**:
   The integration of NLP into AR and VR will further enhance the user experience by allowing natural and seamless voice interactions with

the virtual environment. Users can interact with virtual characters, control virtual objects, or navigate through an immersive world by simply speaking, creating a more intuitive and accessible interface.

Example: Virtual assistants like **Siri**, **Alexa**, and **Google Assistant** have already set a precedent for voice-based interactions. As AI, AR, and VR converge, we'll see even more sophisticated voice interfaces in virtual environments, making it easier to control complex systems using natural speech.

Mixed Reality (MR)

While AR and VR are powerful technologies on their own, the combination of both—**mixed reality (MR)**—is emerging as a game-changing trend. MR allows users to interact with both real-world and virtual objects in real-time, blurring the lines between physical and digital spaces. This convergence of AR and VR will lead to more versatile and realistic immersive experiences, enabling users to interact with digital elements while still maintaining awareness of their physical surroundings.

1. **Real-Time Interaction with Virtual and Physical Worlds**:

MR systems, such as **Microsoft HoloLens**, use advanced sensors, cameras, and computer vision to overlay digital objects onto the real world while tracking users' movements. This allows users to interact with virtual objects as if they were part of their physical environment. MR can be used in a wide range of applications, from training simulations and remote collaboration to interactive product design and virtual gaming.

2. **Collaborative MR Environments**:
   One of the most promising applications of MR is its ability to facilitate collaboration in shared, immersive environments. For example, in a virtual workspace, participants can simultaneously interact with 3D models of products, perform design iterations, and brainstorm ideas, all within a fully interactive digital space.

Example: Spatial, a collaborative MR platform, allows teams to work together in virtual spaces by overlaying 3D models of designs and documents onto the real world. This kind of MR platform is already being used in fields such as architecture and product design, where collaboration and visual interaction with prototypes are critical.

Haptic feedback, or the sense of touch in virtual environments, is another trend that will revolutionize how we experience AR and VR. Current VR systems already use basic haptic controllers to simulate physical sensations, but in the future, we will see much more advanced haptic technologies that can simulate a wider range of textures, pressures, and sensations.

1. **Full-Body Haptics**:
   Companies like **TeslaSuit** are developing full-body haptic suits that provide users with the ability to feel sensations in a more realistic and nuanced way. These suits use a combination of tactile feedback and motion tracking to simulate physical interactions, allowing users to feel everything from the touch of a virtual object to the sensation of running or jumping in a virtual environment.

2. **Sensory Immersion**:
   In addition to haptic feedback, other sensory inputs such as smell, taste, and temperature

are being explored for integration into AR and VR systems. These advancements would create a fully immersive experience where users can perceive all five senses in virtual environments, further blurring the lines between the real world and the digital world.

9.2 The Role of 5G and Edge Computing

For immersive experiences like AR, VR, and MR to reach their full potential, **network connectivity** and **computational power** need to be able to handle the large amounts of data and low latency required. This is where **5G** and **edge computing** come into play. Both of these technologies are poised to play a pivotal role in transforming the way we experience immersive tech.

How Connectivity and Faster Networks Will Shape Immersive Experiences

1. **Ultra-Low Latency with 5G**:
   5G networks offer significantly faster data transfer speeds and much lower latency than previous generations of wireless technology. For immersive experiences, latency is critical,

especially for real-time interaction in VR or MR environments. Any lag between the user's actions and the system's response can disrupt the immersion and cause discomfort, such as motion sickness.

With 5G, users will experience near-instantaneous interactions in AR, VR, and MR environments, making these technologies much more accessible and enjoyable. Whether you are in a VR meeting or playing an immersive game, the responsiveness of the system will drastically improve, providing a seamless experience.

2. **Increased Bandwidth for Data-Heavy Applications**:
   5G's ability to handle massive data throughput is essential for real-time streaming of high-definition VR content, which can require enormous amounts of bandwidth. In addition, 5G will enable cloud-based VR, where users don't need to rely on powerful local hardware. Instead, VR content will be streamed from powerful data centers, reducing the need for expensive, high-performance devices on the consumer side.

Edge Computing and Distributed Processing

While 5G will handle the high-speed connectivity, **edge computing** will tackle the problem of processing power. Edge computing involves processing data closer to the user's location, at the "edge" of the network, rather than relying on a distant data center. This reduces the time it takes to send data to the cloud and back, further lowering latency and improving real-time interactions.

1. **Faster Processing and Real-Time Interaction**: By processing data closer to the user, edge computing can significantly enhance the performance of AR, VR, and MR applications. For example, in a VR game or AR experience, edge computing enables faster rendering and interaction with virtual objects, improving immersion.

2. **Reducing Cloud Dependence**: While cloud computing is essential for many applications, relying on centralized cloud data centers can introduce latency and bandwidth issues. With edge computing, immersive applications will be able to offload computational tasks locally, ensuring a

smoother and more responsive experience without the bottleneck of cloud-based processing.

9.3 The Convergence of AR, VR, and AI

The convergence of AR, VR, and AI is one of the most exciting trends shaping the future of immersive technologies. While each of these technologies has its strengths, their integration will enable even more powerful and transformative experiences.

How Artificial Intelligence Will Revolutionize Immersive Tech

1. **Enhanced Interactivity with AI-Powered Avatars**:
   In both VR and AR environments, AI can be used to create more intelligent and realistic avatars or NPCs (non-playable characters). These avatars can learn from the user's actions, anticipate needs, and provide meaningful interactions, making virtual worlds feel more dynamic and alive. AI-driven characters can adapt in real-time, creating more personalized

experiences based on individual behaviors and preferences.

Example: In VR games, AI-powered NPCs will react to player actions with unprecedented complexity. In the future, these characters could hold conversations with players, learn from previous interactions, and even dynamically alter storylines based on user decisions.

2. **AI in Real-Time Environment Generation**:
   AI will play a crucial role in the real-time creation of environments in immersive technologies. For example, AI could generate new areas in a virtual world based on a player's preferences or the context of their actions. This dynamic content generation allows VR and AR applications to remain engaging and fresh, with virtual environments that constantly evolve based on user interaction.

3. **Intelligent Object Recognition in AR**:
   AI will enhance AR by improving object recognition and scene understanding. This will enable more sophisticated AR applications, where virtual objects can interact with the real world in complex and meaningful ways. AI

algorithms will analyze the real-time environment to understand spatial relationships and context, enabling AR devices to place virtual objects more naturally.

9.4 The Metaverse 2.0: What's Next?

The Metaverse has already gained significant attention, but what does the future hold? The concept of the Metaverse 2.0 is one of continuous evolution, where the digital world becomes even more interconnected, immersive, and complex. This next iteration will likely include more seamless integration between physical and digital worlds, more realistic avatars, and more expansive virtual economies.

The Future of Virtual Worlds and Digital Economies

1. **Hyper-Realistic Digital Worlds**:
   In the Metaverse 2.0, virtual environments will become indistinguishable from the real world. Advances in graphics, AI, and haptics will make these worlds more immersive, with realistic simulations of physical phenomena like lighting, sound, and physics.

2. **Expanded Digital Economies**:
   The Metaverse will see the growth of fully integrated digital economies where virtual assets, currencies, and goods can be traded, sold, or exchanged in real-time. As NFTs and digital currencies become more prevalent, the Metaverse will become a thriving hub for digital commerce, enabling users to own, trade, and create value in virtual environments.

The Integration of Physical and Digital Worlds

1. **Seamless Augmented Reality**:
   In the future, the Metaverse will seamlessly blend the digital and physical worlds through AR. Users will interact with digital objects and information overlaid on the real world using AR glasses or devices, providing a richer, more immersive experience than today's AR.

2. **Hybrid Work and Collaboration**:
   The Metaverse 2.0 will facilitate more sophisticated virtual workplaces, where employees can collaborate, meet, and socialize in fully immersive virtual spaces. This will replace the traditional video conferencing

model, allowing for more engaging and interactive work experiences.

9.5 Hands-On Project: Creating an AI-Powered VR Experience

In this section, we will walk through the process of creating a simple AI-powered VR experience using **Unity** and **TensorFlow**. This project will introduce you to how artificial intelligence can be integrated into VR environments to create dynamic, interactive content.

Step 1: Setting Up the Development Environment

1. **Install Unity**:
   Download and install **Unity**, a popular game engine used for creating both VR and AR applications.

2. **Install TensorFlow**:
   TensorFlow is an open-source AI framework used to build machine learning models. For this project, we'll use TensorFlow to train a model that powers AI avatars in the VR experience.

Step 2: Designing the VR Environment

1. **Create a 3D Environment**:
   Using Unity, create a simple 3D environment, such as a virtual park or room. Import 3D models and set up lighting to create a realistic atmosphere.

2. **Integrate VR Support**:
   Enable VR support in Unity and configure it for platforms such as Oculus Rift or HTC Vive. This will allow you to experience the virtual world using a VR headset.

Step 3: Adding AI to the VR Environment

1. **AI Avatar Interaction**:
   Use TensorFlow to train an AI model that controls avatars in the environment. These avatars should be able to recognize user input, such as gestures or voice commands, and respond accordingly.

2. **Real-Time Feedback**:
   Implement a system where the AI avatars respond to the user's actions, creating a more interactive and engaging experience. For example, an AI avatar could greet the user,

initiate a conversation, or provide feedback based on the user's behavior.

Step 4: Testing and Optimization

1. **Test the VR Experience**:
   Test the VR experience to ensure that the AI avatars respond appropriately and that the VR environment is immersive and smooth.

2. **Optimize Performance**:
   Optimize the VR experience to ensure it runs smoothly on your hardware. Reduce latency, improve frame rates, and ensure that the AI avatars perform efficiently in real-time.

Chapter 10: Practical Applications for AR and VR in Business

10.1 Transforming Business with VR and AR

In the evolving business landscape, immersive technologies such as Augmented Reality (AR) and Virtual Reality (VR) are not just futuristic concepts; they have become integral tools that are reshaping entire industries. From manufacturing and logistics to architecture and construction, VR and AR are improving processes, enhancing efficiency, and creating new opportunities for innovation. In this section, we will explore how these immersive technologies are revolutionizing various sectors, providing businesses with powerful tools for growth and transformation.

Manufacturing and Production

1. **Virtual Prototyping and Design**:
   AR and VR are being used in manufacturing for virtual prototyping, allowing companies to design, test, and refine products without the need for physical prototypes. This reduces both time and cost, enabling faster innovation cycles. Engineers and designers can create 3D models of products and test their functionality in virtual environments before committing to production, minimizing errors and ensuring that the final product is optimized for performance.

Example: **Ford** uses VR to design vehicles in a digital environment. Designers and engineers can walk around, interact with, and modify 3D models of car designs before moving to the physical prototype stage. This saves time and resources while ensuring the design is sound.

2. **Remote Assistance for Maintenance and Repair**:
   AR provides real-time visual guidance for

workers in the field, making it easier to perform maintenance and repairs. Through smart glasses or mobile devices, workers can receive step-by-step instructions overlaid on their environment, enabling them to carry out tasks more accurately and efficiently. This is particularly valuable for industries like aerospace, automotive, and energy, where technicians may be required to maintain complex systems in remote locations.

Example: Boeing uses AR technology to guide workers assembling complex parts of airplanes. By using AR glasses, workers can receive real-time instructions, view 3D models, and avoid errors, improving assembly efficiency and reducing costs.

3. **Training and Simulation**:
   VR is a powerful tool for training employees in manufacturing environments. By simulating real-world tasks and operations, VR allows workers to gain hands-on experience in a controlled, risk-free environment. This is particularly valuable for high-risk industries where safety is paramount, as workers can

practice tasks without the danger of real-world consequences.

Example: Siemens has implemented VR-based training programs for employees to practice machinery operation and complex procedures in a virtual environment. These simulations not only reduce the learning curve but also lower the likelihood of costly mistakes during actual operations.

Logistics and Supply Chain Management

1. **Warehouse Optimization and Management**: AR is used in logistics to enhance warehouse operations. With AR devices, workers can receive real-time information on inventory, picking locations, and order status, streamlining the process of retrieving items. This improves accuracy and speeds up fulfillment, reducing errors and increasing operational efficiency.

Example: DHL has implemented AR glasses for warehouse workers. These glasses provide real-time directions on where to find items, reducing the time spent searching for products and minimizing human error in the fulfillment process.

2. **Supply Chain Visualization**:
   With the help of AR, businesses can visualize their entire supply chain in a more intuitive way. By overlaying digital information on physical assets, AR helps businesses track the movement of goods, identify potential bottlenecks, and optimize inventory management. This improves transparency and reduces operational delays.

Example: UPS uses AR in its logistics operations to visualize package routes and track shipments in real-time. This allows employees to identify potential issues in the supply chain and make decisions based on the most current data.

Architecture and Construction

1. **Building Information Modeling (BIM)**:
   AR and VR are transforming the architecture and construction industries by integrating them into Building Information Modeling (BIM). These immersive technologies allow architects, engineers, and construction teams to visualize designs, simulate building processes, and detect potential issues before construction begins. This reduces errors, improves

collaboration, and accelerates project timelines.

Example: Trimble uses AR to overlay construction plans and architectural designs on the physical construction site. This allows workers to visualize how a building will look and make necessary adjustments in real-time.

2. **Virtual Site Visits and Inspections**:
   With VR, clients, architects, and contractors can conduct virtual site visits and inspections without needing to be physically present. This is particularly beneficial for large-scale projects or remote locations where travel might be time-consuming or costly. VR site tours enable stakeholders to explore the project from any location, offering detailed and interactive walkthroughs.

Example: Autodesk's BIM 360 platform enables virtual site tours and inspections for construction projects, allowing teams to collaborate and resolve issues in virtual spaces before they arise in the real world.

10.2 Immersive Technology for Customer Engagement

The rise of immersive technologies has not only impacted the internal operations of businesses but has also significantly transformed how brands engage with their customers. VR and AR have created new opportunities for marketing, customer service, and building brand loyalty. These technologies offer interactive and personalized experiences that captivate consumers, making them a powerful tool in customer engagement strategies.

AR and VR in Marketing

1. **Immersive Advertising**:
   AR and VR allow brands to create interactive advertisements that engage customers in entirely new ways. Instead of static images or traditional video ads, brands can develop immersive experiences that invite customers to interact with products, services, or brand stories. This type of engagement is more memorable and impactful, fostering a deeper emotional connection between the consumer and the brand.

Example: **Pepsi Max** created an immersive AR experience for commuters at a bus stop. Using a transparent screen and AR technology, the ad made it look like an alien spaceship or tiger was appearing in the street. This unexpected and interactive experience captivated passersby, generating buzz and increasing brand awareness.

2. **Virtual Showrooms and Product Demos**: VR is increasingly being used to create virtual showrooms, where customers can explore products in a highly immersive digital environment. This is particularly beneficial for brands in sectors like automotive, fashion, and real estate, where customers benefit from experiencing products in full detail. Virtual product demos, powered by VR, allow potential buyers to interact with products or simulate usage in a virtual environment, providing a more hands-on experience before making a purchase.

Example: **L'Oreal** has developed an AR beauty app that allows users to try on makeup virtually. By using AR technology, customers can see how different products would look on their skin before making a purchase, enhancing the online shopping experience.

3. **Personalized Experiences**:
   Both AR and VR offer opportunities for personalized customer engagement. Through AR-enabled apps, brands can provide customers with personalized content or recommendations based on their preferences, location, or past purchases. VR allows for a customized virtual shopping experience where users can interact with products and spaces in ways that are tailored to their unique tastes.

Example: **IKEA**'s **IKEA Place** app allows users to virtually place furniture in their homes using AR technology. By seeing how items fit in their spaces, customers can make more informed purchasing decisions, creating a more personalized shopping experience.

Customer Service and Support

1. **Virtual Customer Support**:
   AR and VR are revolutionizing customer service by offering more interactive and immersive support solutions. Using AR, businesses can

provide step-by-step visual guides for troubleshooting or product assembly, eliminating the need for complex written instructions. In VR, businesses can create simulated customer service environments where agents can interact with customers in real time, offering assistance in a more human-like and empathetic manner.

Example: L'Oreal offers virtual customer service experiences, where customers can interact with digital avatars that provide personalized advice on products. These avatars use VR and AR to simulate real-world experiences, creating a more engaging and customer-friendly support system.

2. **Training Customer Service Representatives**: Businesses are using VR simulations to train customer service representatives. These virtual environments simulate real-world interactions, allowing employees to practice resolving customer issues, handling complaints, or conducting sales. This hands-on training prepares agents for a variety of scenarios and improves their ability to interact with customers in real life.

Example: Walmart uses VR to train its employees in customer service, simulating real-world situations such as dealing with difficult customers or handling emergency situations.

10.3 VR for Remote Work and Collaboration

The COVID-19 pandemic accelerated the shift to remote work, and immersive technologies have become invaluable tools for maintaining productivity, collaboration, and employee engagement. VR and AR enable virtual offices, real-time collaboration, and immersive meetings, creating a new paradigm for remote work.

Virtual Offices and Workspaces

1. **Virtual Office Environments**:
   VR enables businesses to create virtual offices where employees can meet, collaborate, and socialize, despite being geographically dispersed. These virtual offices are designed to replicate the look and feel of a traditional office environment, providing employees with a sense

of presence and connection that traditional video calls or messaging platforms cannot.

Example: **Virbela** offers a platform that creates virtual office spaces for remote teams. Employees can use avatars to walk around a 3D office, attend meetings, and interact with colleagues in real time, creating a more immersive and connected remote work experience.

2. **Hybrid Workspaces**:
   In the future, hybrid workplaces, which combine physical and virtual workspaces, will become more common. VR allows employees working remotely to access virtual spaces that mimic physical office settings, providing an immersive environment where collaboration and communication can take place in real time. This will blur the line between in-office and remote work.

Example: **Horizon Workrooms**, developed by Facebook, provides VR spaces where team members can meet, collaborate, and work together using avatars. These spaces replicate the functionality of physical offices and enhance remote collaboration.

1. **Virtual Meetings and Conferences**:
   VR is transforming how businesses conduct meetings, conferences, and presentations. Instead of using standard video conferencing tools, teams can meet in fully immersive virtual spaces where they can interact with presentations, share documents, and collaborate in real time.

Example: **Spatial** is a platform that allows users to hold virtual meetings, collaborate on 3D models, and interact with digital content in real-time. By using VR headsets or AR devices, teams can create a shared virtual space where they can work together regardless of location.

2. **Collaboration on 3D Projects**:
   VR is particularly effective for collaborative work in industries like architecture, design, and engineering. Teams can review 3D models, brainstorm, and provide real-time feedback in immersive virtual environments, making it easier to solve problems and innovate.

Example: **Trimble XR10** is a VR platform designed for the construction industry. It allows project teams to collaborate on 3D building models and simulate construction processes in real time, improving project outcomes and reducing costly errors.

10.4 Hands-On Project: Building a VR Collaboration Space

In this section, we will walk through the process of creating a simple VR collaboration space using **Unity** and the **Oculus SDK**. This will allow you to build an immersive environment where team members can meet and collaborate remotely.

Step 1: Setting Up the Development Environment

1. **Install Unity**:
   Download and install **Unity**, a powerful game engine that supports VR development. Unity provides the tools needed to build immersive environments and integrate VR support.

2. **Install the Oculus SDK**:
   If you're using an **Oculus Rift** or **Oculus Quest**, download and install the **Oculus SDK** for Unity. This SDK enables you to integrate Oculus VR hardware into your project, providing tools for

motion tracking, interaction, and environment rendering.

Step 2: Designing the VR Collaboration Space

1. **Create a Virtual Environment**:
   Start by designing a basic 3D environment in Unity. This will be the virtual office where team members will meet and collaborate. You can use Unity's built-in 3D assets or import models from external programs like **Blender**.

2. **Set Up Interactive Objects**:
   Add interactive objects to the virtual environment, such as whiteboards, desks, and chairs. These objects will enable team members to interact with the space during meetings, brainstorming sessions, and collaboration.

Step 3: Integrating VR Features

1. **Set Up Oculus Integration**:
   Enable Oculus support in Unity and configure the Oculus SDK to track the user's head movements and controller inputs. This will allow users to navigate the virtual environment and interact with objects in real time.

2. **Add Communication Tools**:

   Implement tools for team members to communicate with each other, such as voice chat or text-based messaging. Unity's networking features can be used to allow multiple users to join the virtual space simultaneously.

Step 4: Testing and Optimization

1. **Test the Experience**:

   Test the VR collaboration space to ensure that it functions as intended. Verify that users can navigate the environment, interact with objects, and communicate with others in real-time.

2. **Optimize for Performance**:

   Optimize the VR experience by reducing the polygon count of 3D models, adjusting lighting settings, and optimizing textures to ensure smooth performance on VR headsets.

Chapter 11: Developing with Immersive Technologies

11.1 Choosing the Right Development Tools

When it comes to developing applications for immersive technologies like Virtual Reality (VR) and Augmented Reality (AR), selecting the right development tools is essential for ensuring that your project is successful. The development tools you choose will depend on the type of application you're building, the platform you're targeting, and your personal or team's skill set. The following tools are the most widely used in the immersive technology space and offer comprehensive solutions for building VR and AR applications.

Unity: The Leading Platform for Immersive
Development

Unity is one of the most popular game development
platforms for building both AR and VR applications.
It's widely used due to its flexibility, user-friendly
interface, and support for cross-platform
development. Unity allows developers to build
immersive experiences for a wide range of devices,
including VR headsets (like the Oculus Rift, HTC Vive,
and PlayStation VR), AR platforms (such as ARCore
for Android and ARKit for iOS), and mobile apps.

Why Unity is Ideal for Immersive Development:

1. **Cross-Platform Development**: Unity supports
   multiple platforms, making it easy to develop
   once and deploy to various devices, including
   PC, mobile, and VR/AR hardware.

2. **Asset Store**: Unity's Asset Store provides
   thousands of pre-built assets, including 3D
   models, scripts, environments, and interactive
   elements, which can help speed up
   development.

3. **Support for VR and AR SDKs**: Unity offers
   native support for popular VR and AR SDKs,

such as **Oculus SDK**, **Google ARCore**, and **Apple ARKit**. These SDKs provide tools for motion tracking, gesture recognition, and 3D object placement in AR.

4. **Community and Learning Resources**: Unity has a vast community of developers and a wealth of tutorials, making it easy to find help and resources when building immersive applications.

Example: Many top VR games and applications, such as **Beat Saber** and **VRChat**, were developed using Unity due to its versatile features and strong VR support.

Unreal Engine: High-Quality Visuals and Performance

Unreal Engine, developed by **Epic Games**, is another powerhouse in the world of VR and AR development. Unreal Engine is particularly known for its photorealistic rendering capabilities, making it a preferred choice for developers working on high-quality, graphically intense immersive experiences.

Why Unreal Engine is Ideal for Immersive Development:

1. **Real-Time Graphics Rendering**: Unreal Engine offers some of the best real-time rendering capabilities, enabling developers to create photorealistic environments for VR and AR.

2. **Blueprint Visual Scripting**: Unreal Engine's Blueprint system allows developers to build functionality without writing extensive code. This makes it a great option for designers or artists who want to focus on creativity without diving too deep into programming.

3. **VR/AR Support**: Unreal Engine has built-in support for both VR and AR development, making it easy to create high-quality immersive experiences that are optimized for performance.

4. **Open Source**: Unreal Engine's source code is open and available, allowing developers to fully customize and optimize their applications.

Example: Popular VR games like **The Walking Dead: Saints & Sinners** and high-end AR simulations are developed using Unreal Engine due to its advanced graphical capabilities and performance.

Other Development Platforms

While Unity and Unreal Engine dominate the VR/AR development scene, there are several other tools and platforms worth considering, depending on your specific needs:

1. **Godot**: Godot is an open-source game engine that supports both 2D and 3D game development. It's less resource-intensive than Unity and Unreal Engine, making it ideal for smaller projects or developers looking for a lightweight option.

2. **Vuforia**: A powerful AR development platform, Vuforia is used for building AR experiences for mobile devices, smart glasses, and wearables. It supports image recognition, 3D object tracking, and model-based AR, which makes it ideal for industrial, educational, and entertainment applications.

3. **ARKit/ARCore**: These are platform-specific AR development environments for iOS and Android. While Unity and Unreal Engine are

cross-platform, using ARKit and ARCore directly can give you a more streamlined, native experience for building AR applications on each platform.

Choosing the right development tool ultimately depends on the type of experience you're building, the level of graphical fidelity required, the platform you're targeting, and your team's proficiency with each tool.

11.2 Basic Coding for AR and VR

Understanding the basics of coding is crucial for developing AR and VR applications, whether you're creating interactive experiences, simulations, or games. While both AR and VR development rely heavily on 3D graphics and real-time processing, the coding requirements differ slightly based on the platform and the type of immersive experience you're aiming to create.

Fundamentals of Programming for Immersive Technologies

1. **Understanding Game Development Concepts:**

Both AR and VR development are built on the foundation of game development principles. Familiarity with concepts like **3D transformations**, **scene management**, and **collision detection** is essential for creating engaging immersive experiences. In VR, you'll need to handle issues like head tracking, motion controllers, and user input. For AR, you'll work with **object recognition**, **motion tracking**, and **camera integration**.

2. **C# and Unity**:
   Unity primarily uses **C#** as its programming language. If you're developing VR or AR applications in Unity, you'll need to understand basic C# programming, object-oriented programming (OOP) principles, and how to handle game objects, scenes, and interactions within Unity's environment.

Key Areas to Focus On:

- **VR Input Systems**: Learning how to interact with motion controllers and handle user inputs is crucial for VR development.

- **Scene Setup**: Understanding how to create and manage immersive environments, handle lighting, and design user interfaces (UI) that are intuitive in VR and AR contexts.

- **Physics and Interactivity**: Implementing realistic physics for VR interactions, such as object grabbing, throwing, and colliding with virtual objects, is essential for creating immersive experiences.

3. **Blueprints and Unreal Engine**:
   For developers working with Unreal Engine, **Blueprints** are a visual scripting language that allows you to create functionality without writing code. This is especially helpful for designers or developers who are less familiar with coding. Blueprints are used to handle interactions in VR, trigger events, and manage the flow of gameplay in VR environments.

Key Areas to Focus On:

- **Creating Interactive Elements**: Blueprints can help you create interactive objects, such as buttons, levers, and triggers, which respond to user input in VR.

- ○ **Building Realistic Physics**: Unreal Engine's Blueprint system is used to implement physics-based interactions, such as gravity, friction, and object manipulation, essential for VR environments.

- ○ **Event Handling**: Unreal's Blueprints allow you to handle events, such as the collision of objects or triggering animations, which are critical for creating immersive VR and AR experiences.

4. **AR-Specific Coding Considerations**:
In AR, you will be interacting with real-world environments, requiring a different set of considerations compared to VR. AR development typically involves using camera feeds, tracking systems, and placing virtual objects over real-world views. Programming in AR includes managing spatial anchors, handling object recognition, and ensuring that virtual content is properly aligned with real-world environments.

Key Areas to Focus On:

- o **Spatial Mapping and Scene Understanding**: Using AR SDKs like ARCore (for Android) or ARKit (for iOS), you'll learn how to map real-world surfaces, detect objects, and anchor virtual objects in the real world.

- o **Marker-based and Markerless AR**: Implementing both marker-based AR (where images or QR codes are used to trigger content) and markerless AR (where virtual objects are placed directly in the environment based on camera data) is essential for effective AR experiences.

Tools for Coding in AR and VR Development

1. **Visual Studio**: Visual Studio is the primary IDE (Integrated Development Environment) for Unity development. It integrates with Unity and supports C# for scripting VR/AR applications.

2. **Xcode**: If you're developing AR applications for iOS with ARKit, Xcode is required for building and running applications on Apple devices.

3. **Android Studio**: For ARCore-based AR development on Android, Android Studio is the primary development environment, supporting Java or Kotlin for programming AR applications.

4. **Blender**: Blender is a popular open-source 3D modeling tool that can be used to create assets for both VR and AR applications. You can export models from Blender and import them directly into Unity or Unreal Engine.

11.3 Creating Interactive Experiences

One of the core features of immersive technologies is interaction—whether it's moving through a VR environment, manipulating virtual objects, or interacting with virtual characters in AR. The success of these experiences depends heavily on how well interactivity is implemented and how intuitive it feels for users.

Game Mechanics in VR and AR

1. **Understanding Interaction Mechanics**:
   In both VR and AR, interaction mechanics play a pivotal role in how users experience the technology. This includes not only physical

interaction (like grabbing objects or pressing buttons) but also virtual interactions (like changing the environment, triggering actions, or altering gameplay).

Key Interaction Types:

- ○ **Gestures**: In VR and AR, users can interact with the virtual world through gestures. VR headsets like the **Oculus Rift** or **HTC Vive** allow for hand tracking, which can be used for precise gesture recognition and interaction with virtual elements.

- ○ **Voice Commands**: Some VR applications use voice recognition as a primary input method, allowing users to control virtual objects or navigate through a virtual environment with voice commands.

- ○ **Eye Tracking**: Advanced VR systems like the **Varjo XR-1** use eye-tracking technology, allowing for more natural interactions, such as selecting objects by simply looking at them.

2. **Immersive Navigation**:
Navigation within VR and AR is critical to ensuring that users are able to move through immersive environments without feeling lost or disoriented. There are several methods for handling navigation in VR, including teleportation, walking, and joystick-based movement.

   o **Teleportation**: Teleportation is a common navigation method in VR, especially in applications that involve large environments. It allows users to point to a location and instantly "teleport" there, avoiding the issue of motion sickness.

   o **Walking and Joystick Movement**: For applications that aim for a more realistic experience, walking and joystick controls are used, allowing users to navigate freely through a virtual space. This is common in VR games or simulations that require full-body movement.

3. **Interactive Storytelling and AI**:
Interactive storytelling is another area where immersive technologies shine. With AI

integration, VR and AR environments can change dynamically based on user decisions, making the experience feel personalized and responsive. This is especially powerful in gaming, where user choices can influence the outcome of the narrative.

Example: AI-driven storylines in VR applications like **The Walking Dead: Saints & Sinners** make the game world responsive to player actions, allowing for a more customized and immersive experience.

11.4 Hands-On Project: Building Your First AR Game

In this section, we will walk through the steps of creating a basic AR game using **Unity** and **ARFoundation**. This hands-on project will give you the fundamentals of developing interactive AR experiences that respond to the real world.

Step 1: Setting Up the Development Environment

1. **Install Unity**:
   Download and install the latest version of Unity. Create a new Unity project using the **AR template**.

2. **Install ARFoundation**:
   ARFoundation is Unity's cross-platform framework for AR development. Install it via Unity's Package Manager. ARFoundation supports both **ARCore** (Android) and **ARKit** (iOS).

Step 2: Creating the AR Game Environment

1. **Set Up the AR Camera**:
   In Unity, the AR camera will replace the standard camera used in non-AR games. This camera interacts with the device's sensors and renders virtual content based on real-world interactions.

2. **Add AR Elements**:
   Using ARFoundation, you can add real-world objects for interaction. For example, you can place virtual items or targets in the real world using **plane detection** or **image tracking**.

Step 3: Implementing Interactive Gameplay

1. **Touch Interaction**:
   Implement basic touch interactions in the game. When a user taps on the screen, the game should spawn a virtual object in the real

world. The player should be able to interact with it, such as tapping on an object to "collect" it or trigger an animation.

2. **Collision Detection**:
   Use Unity's physics engine to detect when virtual objects collide with real-world surfaces or other virtual objects. This will create a more engaging and realistic interaction.

Step 4: Testing the AR Game

1. **Test on Device**:
   Once your game is ready, test it on a physical device. Make sure the AR elements are anchored correctly to real-world surfaces and the interactions work as expected.

2. **Optimize for Performance**:
   Optimize your AR game by reducing the polygon count of 3D models, improving lighting settings, and using efficient textures to ensure smooth performance on mobile devices.

Chapter 12: Preparing for the Future: Opportunities and Careers in Immersive Tech

12.1 The Growing Market for Immersive Tech

The market for immersive technologies—encompassing **Virtual Reality (VR)**, **Augmented Reality (AR)**, and **Web3**—is rapidly expanding. These technologies are no longer confined to niche markets or entertainment; they are making a substantial impact across a range of industries, opening up a vast number of opportunities for both businesses and professionals. From healthcare and education to real estate and entertainment, AR, VR, and Web3 are reshaping how companies operate and how consumers engage with products and services.

Job Opportunities in Immersive Tech

As the demand for immersive technologies grows, industries are increasingly looking for skilled professionals who can develop, design, and manage these advanced experiences. The immersive tech job market spans a diverse set of roles, including software developers, designers, product managers, and AI experts. Let's take a look at some of the most prominent sectors where immersive tech is driving significant change.

1. **Healthcare**:
   The healthcare industry has quickly embraced immersive technologies to enhance training, treatment, and patient engagement. VR is being used for surgical simulations, physical rehabilitation, and pain management, while AR is helping surgeons visualize complex procedures in real-time. The integration of **Web3** technologies through blockchain is also

being explored for secure medical record-keeping and patient data management.

Key Opportunities:

- VR/AR developers for medical simulation software

- UI/UX designers for healthcare apps and tools

- Data analysts for Web3 healthcare applications (blockchain-based health records)

2. **Education and Training**:
   The education sector is experiencing a revolution through AR and VR. Virtual classrooms and immersive simulations enable more interactive learning experiences. VR is helping students understand complex subjects through experiential learning, while AR overlays digital information on real-world objects, facilitating hands-on training and tutorials.

Key Opportunities:

- VR/AR content creators for educational programs

- Instructional designers for immersive learning environments

- Web3 developers for building decentralized learning platforms

3. **Retail and E-commerce**:
Retailers are increasingly leveraging AR and VR to offer enhanced shopping experiences. Virtual showrooms, try-before-you-buy applications, and immersive customer service platforms are improving both online and in-store shopping experiences. Web3's potential in retail is also being explored, particularly with NFTs for digital goods and blockchain for secure transactions.

Key Opportunities:

- AR/VR developers for retail apps and virtual storefronts

- Marketing professionals specializing in immersive tech campaigns

- Web3 consultants for NFT-based retail projects

4. **Entertainment and Media**:
Entertainment has long been a driving force for

AR and VR innovation, with the gaming industry being one of the earliest adopters. As immersive storytelling and game mechanics evolve, the entertainment industry is also embracing AR for live experiences and Web3 technologies for creating decentralized virtual worlds. The use of **NFTs** and **crypto** is opening up new possibilities for monetizing digital content.

Key Opportunities:

- VR game developers and designers
- 3D artists for immersive visual content in AR/VR environments
- Web3 project managers for virtual economies and NFT marketplaces

5. **Manufacturing and Industry**:
Manufacturing industries are using AR for real-time instructions and remote assistance, while VR is aiding in design prototyping and employee training. The integration of Web3 in manufacturing is emerging, with blockchain being utilized for supply chain tracking and product authenticity.

Key Opportunities:

- AR/VR developers for manufacturing simulation tools

- Engineers working with immersive training and design platforms

- Blockchain experts for supply chain transparency and product tracking

6. **Real Estate**:

The real estate sector has adopted VR for virtual tours, helping potential buyers or renters explore properties remotely. AR is being used to visualize changes or renovations in existing properties. Web3, through NFTs, is even being explored for creating digital ownership and transactions in virtual real estate.

Key Opportunities:

- VR developers for real estate applications

- AR specialists for home renovation visualization apps

- Blockchain developers for virtual property transactions and NFTs

7. **Corporate Collaboration and Remote Work**: As more companies shift to remote work, VR and AR are creating opportunities for virtual offices and collaborative workspaces. Virtual reality allows teams to meet in fully immersive environments, while AR enhances productivity by overlaying key information or tutorials on physical objects.

Key Opportunities:

- VR collaboration tool developers
- AR software engineers for workplace productivity tools
- Product managers for virtual meeting platforms

Industries Embracing Web3

While AR and VR are capturing much of the spotlight, **Web3** is also gaining traction across multiple industries. Web3 is creating decentralized applications (DApps) and enabling new business models based on **blockchain, cryptocurrencies**, and **smart contracts**. Key industries adopting Web3 technologies include finance (DeFi), supply chain management, gaming, art, and real estate. The rise of

NFTs (non-fungible tokens) and decentralized autonomous organizations (DAOs) are a major driving force behind this transformation.

12.2 Career Paths in Immersive Tech

As immersive technologies continue to evolve and expand across industries, a wide range of career paths are opening up for skilled professionals. The immersive tech sector is multidisciplinary, involving areas like software development, design, product management, and even business strategy. Below are some of the key career roles in the immersive tech industry:

1. VR/AR Developer

Role Overview: Developers in the immersive tech space are responsible for building the underlying software and applications that power VR and AR experiences. These roles often require strong programming skills and experience with game engines like **Unity** and **Unreal Engine**.

- **Skills Required**:

- Proficiency in **C#** (for Unity) or **C++** (for Unreal Engine)

- Understanding of **3D modeling, motion tracking**, and **object recognition**

- Knowledge of VR/AR hardware integration (e.g., Oculus, HoloLens)

- Experience with **multiplayer networking, real-time rendering**, and **game mechanics**

- **Potential Job Titles**:

  - VR Developer

  - AR Developer

  - Unity Developer

  - Unreal Engine Developer

2. VR/AR Designer

Role Overview: Designers in the VR and AR space focus on creating the immersive environments, interactive elements, and user interfaces that make AR/VR applications engaging and functional. They are responsible for both the visual aspects and the user experience design of immersive projects.

- **Skills Required:**

  - Expertise in **3D design software** (e.g., **Blender, Maya, ZBrush**)

  - Experience with **UI/UX design** and interaction design principles

  - Understanding of **real-time rendering** and visual effects in VR/AR

  - Familiarity with VR/AR hardware and the limitations of different devices

- **Potential Job Titles:**

  - 3D Environment Artist

  - VR/AR UX/UI Designer

  - Interactive Designer

  - VR Game Designer

3. Product Manager

Role Overview: A product manager in the immersive tech space oversees the entire lifecycle of an immersive tech product, from concept to launch. They manage the vision, roadmap, and development process, ensuring that the product meets the needs of the business and the user.

- **Skills Required**:
    - Strong project management and **agile development** skills
    - Understanding of VR/AR technologies and user experience
    - Ability to gather and analyze user feedback
    - Knowledge of **market trends** and **business strategy** for immersive technologies

- **Potential Job Titles**:
    - VR/AR Product Manager
    - Immersive Technology Project Manager
    - Product Owner for Web3 applications

4. 3D Artist for VR/AR

Role Overview: Artists in the immersive tech industry create the visual components for VR and AR experiences. This includes 3D modeling, texturing, lighting, and rendering to ensure that digital objects and environments look realistic and fit seamlessly into the immersive world.

- **Skills Required**:
  - Proficiency in **3D modeling tools** like **Blender, 3ds Max**, or **Maya**
  - Strong understanding of **lighting, texturing**, and **real-time rendering**
  - Ability to optimize 3D models for VR/AR hardware
  - Creativity and attention to detail for designing interactive 3D assets
- **Potential Job Titles**:
  - 3D Environment Artist
  - VR/AR 3D Modeler
  - Texture Artist for VR/AR
  - VR Animation Specialist

12.3 How to Stay Ahead in the Industry

Given the rapid evolution of immersive technologies, professionals in the field must stay current with the latest trends, tools, and techniques. Below are several strategies to help you stay ahead in the competitive world of immersive tech.

Continuing Education

1. **Online Courses and Certifications**:
   Many platforms offer online courses and certifications to help you expand your knowledge of immersive technologies. **Udemy, Coursera, edX**, and **Pluralsight** all offer courses on Unity, Unreal Engine, ARCore, ARKit, Web3 development, and more. Certifications can help you build credibility and demonstrate your expertise to potential employers.

2. **University Programs**:
   Universities are increasingly offering degree programs in immersive technologies. Look for programs that focus on game development, AR/VR design, and immersive computing. A formal education can provide a strong foundation in both the technical and creative aspects of immersive tech.

3. **Workshops and Meetups**:
   Immersive tech communities often host workshops, hackathons, and meetups. These events are a great way to stay up-to-date with

the latest developments and network with other professionals in the field. Participating in these events can also provide hands-on experience and exposure to cutting-edge technologies.

Certifications and Building a Portfolio

1. **Immersive Tech Certifications**:
   Several industry-recognized certifications can boost your credentials. For instance, Unity offers **Unity Certified Developer** and **Unity Certified Expert** programs. Similarly, Unreal Engine provides certifications for developers working with its platform. Web3-focused certifications like **Blockchain Developer** or **NFT Certified Developer** are valuable for those working in the decentralized space.

2. **Building a Portfolio**:
   Your portfolio is the key to showcasing your skills and getting hired. A portfolio should include:

   - **Completed projects**: Demonstrating your hands-on skills is crucial. Show off VR/AR games, interactive simulations, or Web3 applications you've developed.

- ○ **Interactive demos**: Including playable versions of your projects or video walkthroughs can help potential employers experience your work firsthand.

- ○ **Code samples**: If you're a developer, host your code on GitHub and link to it in your portfolio. This will give employers insight into your coding style and problem-solving abilities.

3. **Personal Projects**:
   Always keep learning by building personal projects. This can help you experiment with new technologies, refine your skills, and create portfolio pieces that are unique to your interests.

Networking and Industry Involvement

1. **Industry Conferences and Meetups**:
   Immersive tech conferences like **AWE (Augmented World Expo)**, **SIGGRAPH**, and **GDC (Game Developers Conference)** are great opportunities to network with industry leaders, stay informed about new trends, and discover new tools and platforms.

2. **Online Communities**:
   Engage with online communities on platforms like **Reddit**, **Stack Overflow**, and **Discord**, where you can discuss immersive tech, ask questions, and get feedback from other professionals.

3. **Collaboration and Mentorship**:
   Collaborating with others on open-source projects or joining mentorship programs can provide valuable experience, foster learning, and help you gain insights from experienced professionals in the field.

12.4 Hands-On Project: Creating Your Portfolio for Immersive Tech Careers

In this section, we'll guide you through the process of creating a standout portfolio that showcases your VR, AR, or Web3 projects to potential employers or clients. Your portfolio is your chance to demonstrate your skills, creativity, and technical expertise, so it's essential to make it compelling and easy to navigate.

Step 1: Select Your Best Projects

Choose 3-5 of your best projects to feature in your portfolio. Include a mix of different types of work—such as interactive AR experiences, VR games, and Web3 applications—to showcase your versatility. Ensure that these projects highlight your skills in both development and design.

Step 2: Document Your Work

For each project, provide a detailed explanation, including:

- **Objective**: What was the goal of the project? What problem did it solve or what experience did it offer?

- **Technology Used**: Detail the tools and platforms you used (Unity, Unreal Engine, ARCore, etc.) and why you chose them for this project.

- **Process**: Outline the steps you took to complete the project. This can include design iterations, challenges faced, and how you solved them.

- **Outcome**: Describe the final product. Did it meet the goals you set for the project? Include any user feedback or success metrics (if available).

To make your portfolio stand out:

- **Use visuals**: Include screenshots, GIFs, or videos that demonstrate the interactive elements of your work. For VR projects, consider including video walkthroughs or 360-degree images.

- **Provide live demos**: Host your projects on a website or platform where potential employers can try out the experience themselves (e.g., a playable VR game demo, an interactive AR app on mobile, or a Web3 DApp).

Step 4: Create an Online Portfolio

Choose a platform to host your

portfolio, such as **GitHub Pages**, **Behance**, or your own personal website. Make sure your website is easy to navigate and visually appealing. Include sections for your projects, resume, contact information, and any additional skills or certifications.